THANKS FOR THE MIRACLES

[signature]

You Gotta Be Kidding!

The Story of
Children's Miracle
Network Hospitals

Mick Shannon

For the Kids

Published by Mick Shannon
cmnhospitalsfounder@gmail.com
801-243-2426

ISBN 978-0-578-64230-7

Cover and book design by Daniel Ruesch Design
www.danielruesch.net

Cover Photo: Mick Shannon with Ciarlo Liples.
Ciarlo was born at Children's hospital of Philadelphia in the Special Delivery Unit in August of 2010 with Spina Bifida (myelomeningocele) and Hydrocephalus. Ciarlo is paralyzed from the hips down but he doesn't let that slow him down! Ciarlo is a smart, funny, charismatic and loving boy that brings a ray of sunshine to all who meet him! He loves playing wheelchair basketball with his team out of Philadelphia, the Katie's Komets! He wants to be a child life specialist when he grows up. Ciarlo was proud to be a national representative for Children's Miracle Network for 2019 where he was able to raise awareness for Spina Bifida, Hydrocephalus and childhood cancer. Ciarlo's older brother, Dominic passed away at 8 years old from Glioblastoma in 2016.

Dedicated to
the Shannon children:
Merrilee
Amy
RJ
Matthew
Riley
Sheridan
Kyle
and Ryan

Contents

Joe Lake, Marie Osmond, and Bill Marriott

Foreword

The Marriott family's history of supporting children's hospitals goes back to Alice Marriott's mother, who worked at Primary Children's Hospital in Salt Lake City in the early 1900s. Her work at the hospital involved meeting sick and injured children at the train station and to take care of them when their parents couldn't afford to be there for them.

Children's Miracle Network is an outstanding organization that we have proudly supported from the very beginning. When Joe (Lake) and Marie (Osmond) asked me to be a corporate sponsor I said "Absolutely! That's one thing I would love to do." It goes back to my personal experience when my daughter Debbie became one of the first patients to undergo open heart surgery in 1962 at the age of five. Marriott International is proud to be the longest standing corporate partner for Children's Miracle Network Hospitals. Our passion for helping sick and injured children comes from our core values. Our associates and guests often have personal connections to their local children's hospitals. We are delighted to celebrate 37 years supporting Children's Miracle Network Hospitals and look forward to many more years to come. Over the years our associates and guests have donated over $140 million for the kids.

Bill Marriott
Chairman
Marriott Corporation

....

When I look back at the history of RE/MAX, the real estate company my wife Gail and I founded in 1973, I see a number of key moments where the right idea hit at exactly the right time—and became instrumental in defining what our brand is today.

One of those moments occurred in 1992, when we became a corporate sponsor of Children's Miracle Network.

It was a magical fit. When the partnership was announced at the RE/MAX Convention that year, our people—entrepreneurs invested in building relationships and having a meaningful impact in their communities—were all-in from the very start.

The CMN alliance provided a structure to many of the things agents were already doing – connecting with homebuyers and sellers and creating goodwill by serving others in a variety of ways. Tying those activities to an effort that supports local kids, local families and local hospitals made perfect sense.

Through a frenetic live auction and several other fundraisers, RE/MAX agents donated generously at that 1992 convention in Atlanta. More importantly, they took the concept back to their offices and got others as fired up about it as they were. The passion spread throughout our organization, and RE/MAX agents and brokerages began raising money through every

Mick Shannon with 1988 Miracle Child, Alvaro Garza, Jr.

Miracle Under the Ice

The water was freezing cold in the Red River that day. It was Friday, December 4, 1987, fourteen minutes after four o'clock in the afternoon. Eleven-year-old Alvaro Garza Jr., his little brother Joey, and two of their friends were playing along the banks of the river, horsing around in the snow, when they came upon a dead squirrel lying frozen on the ground. One of the boys picked up the squirrel and flung it toward the river. It skidded along the ice and wound up seventy-five yards beyond the bank, lying motionless atop the frozen water. The boys dared each other to go get it. It was a cold day at the start of a cold winter in Moorhead, Minnesota, and Fargo, North Dakota—the twin border towns that straddle the Red River. The river was frozen solid along its edges. But toward the middle the current still flowed lazily in icy chunks.

Alvaro took the dare. He walked cautiously onto the ice and out toward the squirrel, inching closer, so far, so good, until suddenly the ice gave way and he plunged out of sight. The boys, horrified, ran to the Garza's house nearby. Alvaro's mother dialed 9-1-1. Within four minutes the Fargo Fire Department was on the scene with two boats they pushed into the frigid water. The men began breaking the ice and probing with long poles. Visibility was a few inches at most. Their hope was that their probes would find the boy before it was too late. Hope was wearing thing, and most figured it already was too late.

Word quickly spread. A crowd gathered beside the river. News trucks and television cameras arrived to document the scene as the minutes seemed like hours. A half hour went by. Forty minutes. Dusk was giving way to dark. On the shore, first responders whispered about shutting down the search until morning lest anyone working in the boats fall into the river and make a desperate situation even worse.

Then, just as the clock approached five o'clock, a probe hit a solid object. "Wait a minute, I think I've got something," exclaimed a fireman.

They'd found Alvaro.

Within seconds, the boy's purple, bloated body was lifted into a boat. A rescuer said it was like picking up a giant water balloon. A waiting ambulance rushed the unconscious boy to St. Luke's Hospital in Fargo. He had been in the water for forty-five minutes.

Clinically, Alvaro was dead. The life support machines at St. Luke's registered no heartbeat, no respiration, no brain activity. Just flat lines. His body temperature had plunged to 77 degrees. But the boy had kept his head above water for a few minutes before he slipped underneath the surface, giving the body time enough to cool and reduce its need for oxygen, helping prevent irreversible damage to organs and cell tissues. Hoping against hope, the team of physicians at St. Luke's, led by Dr. William Norberg, used a heart-lung bypass machine to force in air and push out water and slowly warm the blood at the rate of one degree every five minutes.

Just after six o'clock Alvaro's heart started beating. At midnight he moved his feet. At two o'clock in the morning he responded to touch...

...Seventeen days later, four days before Christmas, Alvaro Garza walked out of the hospital under his own power. He was known as "The Christmas Miracle."

St. Luke's held a press conference the day of Alvaro's release. All the major news networks were there. For two and a half weeks, Alvaro's story had riveted America, and much of the world. Millions had prayed and pulled and hoped and begged for his recovery. No one had prayed and pulled and hoped and begged harder or followed the story more closely than those of us at Children's Miracle Network. The story had become intimately personal. St. Luke's was one of our member hospitals, and the critical bypass machine that warmed Alvaro's heart had been purchased with money directly donated to St. Luke's through CMN fundraising. As Alvaro recovered, whenever the TV cameras focused in on the machine, there on the side, prominently displayed, was the CMN balloon logo.

When Alvaro and his younger brother Joey emerged from the hospital corridor into the press conference, both were wearing sweatshirts with CHILDREN'S MIRACLE NETWORK spelled out below our distinctive balloon logo. St. Luke's had decided to have the boys wear the CMN shirts. When I asked Dr. Norberg why they chose to do that, he said, "Because that machine saved his life."

The boys' smiles lit up the room, for all the world to see. No public relations strategy imaginable could have raised that kind of positive publicity.

Five months later, we invited Alvaro and his family to Disneyland for our annual Memorial Day Weekend telethon. As a featured part of the show, we always included children who had been treated, or were being treated, at member children's hospitals. Nothing said who we were and what we were all about better than that. We called them our Miracle Kids, and produced powerful videos to tell their stories.

When we began Children's Miracle Network in 1983 there had been pushback by many hospitals and mostly physicians in the medical community at using "miracle" as part of our name. People feared the word might carry a negative connotation; that we might not be taken seriously; that we could offend or scare some hospitals away; that healthcare was a matter of sound, solid science. Miracles didn't have anything to do with it.

But we were stubborn and stuck with the name. Then along came Alvaro Garza Jr., and many, many more with stories just like his. Stories that warm the heart and defy the odds.

"When a lot of people try really hard and care very much, maybe that's what a miracle truly is," one of the rescuers who helped pull Alvaro Garza Jr. from the Red River said to the media. No one who was there would argue with that, or that Miracle shouldn't be our middle name.

Mick Shannon (cute huh?)

....

CHAPTER ONE

It's a Wonderful Life

Okay, here we go. This was the ride of a lifetime. I knew exactly where I was going and what I was going to do with my life. I loved history, I loved politics. In fact my senior year in high school we were given an assignment to write an essay on the presidential race between Nixon and McGovern. I wrote that Nixon would intentionally stab you in the back, and McGovern would mistakenly stab you in the back. Pretty insightful huh?

After studying history and political science in college, I was going to be a history teacher and football coach. That was the plan. It made all the sense in the world. I majored in history in college, and football, well, football was my first love. For a boy growing up in Big Spring, Texas, it was practically impossible not to love football. Nothing was more revered in the Lone Star state, not even oil. The head football coach at Big Spring High School made $60,000 a year, to give you some kind of an idea. In 1967.

I was fourteen when my dad moved us to west Texas, specifically to Big Spring, a town located one hundred miles south of Lubbock, eighty miles west of Abilene, and forty miles east of Midland (in west Texas, that translates to right next door). Midland and the neighboring city of Odessa are the oil towns where future president George H.W. Bush raised another future president, George W. Bush. Odessa Permian High School was featured in "Friday Night Lights," the bestselling book and subsequent movie/TV series about high school football. If you've never experienced what can only be described as a phenomenon, I can't begin to adequately communicate the importance of high school football in Texas. The entire town shuts down on game night. The stadium at Big Spring High School held twelve thousand people—in a city with a population of twenty-five thousand. The stadium at San Angelo held twenty thousand. Everything is beyond big, including the players. I went out for the team for the first time in ninth grade, shortly after moving to Texas, and remember walking onto the field and seeing this guy who was about six-two and two hundred-thirty pounds with a little facial hair. I thought he was one of the coaches. Turned out, he was our fullback.

I'm not trying to represent that I was a star for the Big Spring High School Steers. The truth is, I rarely saw any actual playing time. Although I was a standout practice player. I was just five-eight and one hundred thirty pounds, but I never backed down so I was the perfect tackling dummy. When the coaches thought guys were slacking off or dogging it during drills they would call out in my direction, "Show 'em how it's done Shannon, smack 'em in the mouth." And I'd smack 'em in the mouth. Then, as a result of being tough, ultra competitive, or just plain stupid, I'd get smacked back. The coaches loved it. And I loved it. For me, the positives far outweighed any negatives. The values and principles I learned from Texas high school football have stayed with me all my life. I was taught great lessons in terms of teamwork, sacrifice, hard work, perseverance, and never giving up no matter what—the kinds of things the sport teaches so well. And after every road game the entire team went to a nice restaurant and we all got a chicken fried steak dinner.

The first years of my life were spent in Iowa. I was born in Sioux City at St. Luke's Hospital (later to become a part of the CMN family) on January 27, 1949—right in the middle of the baby boom. After I arrived, my parents, Paul and Marjorie Shannon, had three more boys, my brothers Dennis, Tim, and Leonard, and finally a girl, my baby sister Deb, who didn't come along until after we'd made the move to Texas.

My dad was a day laborer who grew up during the Great Depression. For our family, the depression more or less continued. We had next to nothing and my father's work was sporadic at best. In Iowa, we lived in a little two-room house outside Sioux City on a farm where my dad did farm work. At night my brothers and I would sleep crossways on one double bed, all four of us.

As far back as I can remember, I worked doing *something* to try and earn money. I delivered papers and shoveled snow and mowed lawns all summer and then my mother would use the money to buy school clothes for all us boys. When I got old enough, after we moved to Texas, I worked at a gas station and managed a trampoline park. As a high school senior, when football season was over, I worked the night shift at the state mental hospital, from 11 to 7. I was in a cage, eighty-four patients were in one big room, bunk after bunk. If I needed help I would call for the roving attendants, who would come for whatever was needed. When patients acted up they were put on a list for shock treatment the next morning. One morning I went down to observe shock treatment. I never, ever put anyone on the list again.

After my shift at the mental hospital I went straight to school.

Paul and Marjorie Shannon had their hands full and I knew it, so the day after I graduated high school I lightened their load by stuffing everything I owned into the '57 Chevrolet I'd managed to buy with my savings, waved so long to Texas, and set out for Seattle. I'd heard there were plenty of job opportunities in the Pacific Northwest—and, full disclosure, a girl I knew was moving there with her parents and that might have had something to do with it too.

I'd learned carpentry in a class in high school and soon discovered that the Pacific Northwest was, as advertised, booming with employment opportunities. Boeing was expanding significantly in Seattle and a building boom was going on. All you had to do was drive around and find a new housing development, seek out the foreman, and he'd say, "You're hired!" I'd brought my little sixteen-ounce hammer with me from Texas. The first foreman I worked with took one look at it and threw it in the trees. Then he handed me a forty-two-ounce corrugated hammer to frame with. That night I couldn't raise my arm.

I made a dime per square foot framing houses. The entire house was pre-cut, which made it easy once you got the hang of it. I hooked up with two guys who had driven up from California in an El Camino. Lunch for those guys was a six-pack. They worked hard and they worked fast. The three of us got so we could frame a house in a day. By the end of the year I'd saved $12,000, enough to send me off to college. In the fall of 1968 I enrolled at Ricks Junior College in Rexburg, Idaho.

I chose Ricks primarily because it was owned and operated by The Church of Jesus Christ of Latter-day Saints, the religion I belong to. My parents weren't active churchgoers but my grandmother in Iowa, Emma Barnes, was. She made sure I was baptized (in the YWCA pool) and took me and my brothers to church when we were little, living in Iowa.

At Ricks College, I worked on a potato farm and processing plant owned by Paul Nedrow and got my associates degree in two years. Paul allowed me to work all the hours I wanted, not only paying my tuition but again saving money. Next I moved on to Ricks's big brother, Brigham Young University in Provo, Utah, to continue my education. I framed houses and apartment buildings for two more years, and majored, as I said, in history and political science. By 1973 I'd fulfilled all my credits to graduate from BYU. All that was left was a quarter of student teaching to get my teaching certificate.

I did my student teaching at Midvale Junior High School in the Salt Lake City suburbs. When you go into an eighth grade class as the student teacher, they might as well put a sign on you that says "Abuse the new guy." My first day solo the kids decided to take advantage, standing in the windowsills, slapping yardsticks on the desk, running wild. This was before cell phones or they all would have been on their phones as well.

In my best Texas football voice I said, "Sit your asses down right now!" For good measure, I sent one of the more enthusiastic rioters to the office. And that took care of that. I was pretty proud of myself, I have to say. I could do this, I felt. Bring it on.

I chose to ignore the comment my academic adviser at BYU made in my exit interview. "I don't think you ought to be a teacher," she said, "because you're too grumpy in the morning." I thought, "What's she talking about; I'm grumpy all day long." Not much you can do about that. As soon as student teaching was over, I started applying for full time teaching jobs.

While I was ambitious, my timing couldn't have been much worse. Nineteen seventy-three was not a good year to want to be a school teacher. Supply was significantly higher than demand. Apparently, the word of me taming that classroom at Midvale Junior High did not spread like I hoped. I got rejection letter after rejection letter—and that was just from the schools that bothered to respond. I had exactly one interview at a Salt Lake-area school district. I didn't get the job.

Finally, I did receive one offer; sight unseen. The school district in Bend, Oregon, was looking for a history teacher. They looked at my resume. Was I interested in moving to the middle of Oregon? I don't think so. For whatever reason, it did not feel right. I still wanted to be a teacher, just not there. Maybe if they'd said something about also coaching football.

But I had to find employment. The bills weren't paying themselves.

In survival mode, I started going to the job placement center at BYU to see what employment opportunities were being posted. In the pre-internet era, employers advertised by putting notices on three-by-five cards and hanging them on the placement center bulletin board.

One day I noticed a new posting. The March of Dimes was looking for an executive director for its Idaho operation. Nothing in my training qualified me for working for a nonprofit charity. It wasn't history, politics, or football; it wasn't house framing or potato farming or mowing lawns or manning the graveyard shift at the state mental hospital from 11 to 7

I put my name down anyway—at the bottom of an already sizeable list. Desperate times call for desperate moves. And what could it hurt? I was young. I was flexible. I had a good business sense (I always knew you had to make more than you spend.). I was ready for an adventure. But never in my wildest dreams could I have imagined the unbelievable journey I was about to begin or where it would lead—and how grateful I would be for not accepting that offer to teach in Bend, Oregon. Had I taken that position, nothing that follows here would have ever happened. **No Children's Miracle Network!**

President Franklin Roosevelt, himself a victim of polio, started the precursor to the March of Dimes in 1938. He is meeting here with March of Dimes executive Basil O'Connor.

....

CHAPTER TWO

That Little Orange Toyota

Felix Montes was the Northwest Regional Director for the March of Dimes. Idaho was part of his region. He came to the BYU campus shortly after the notice went up on the bulletin board to interview the hopefuls. I found out later that he liked BYU graduates because he'd had success with them in the past, which bode well for me. Our interview went well. We had an easy connection. When Felix asked if he could come over to my apartment and meet my wife, I took that as a good sign. Then he asked me to step out on the porch and, just like that, offered me the job as executive director of the Idaho March of Dimes. Cool, I thought. Common sense business practices and principles would carry the day.

He didn't offer the position outright. I'd first be on probation. "Let's get you up to Boise for a few weeks," he said, "and see how it goes." I could drive back and forth on the weekends to be with my family. If all went well, we'd move to Boise and make it permanent.

To get started, I went to the Toyota dealer in Provo and paid $2,170 for a brand new 1973 Toyota Corolla. The payment was $81 a month. It had a stick shift, cloth seats, a radio, and got thirty miles to the gallon. And it was orange. No one would have a hard time seeing me coming.

The March of Dimes put me up at a brand new Rodeway Inn in Boise and took care of my meals. It was my first time staying in a hotel, my first time eating in nice restaurants on an expense account, my first time driving around in a new car and getting reimbursed twenty-one cents a mile. There wasn't much about my new circumstances that didn't agree with me.

After five weeks, I got the green light and the March of Dimes hired a moving van and moved us to Boise. We rented a two-bedroom apartment not far from the office and settled in.

I couldn't have hand picked a better place to start a career in the not-for-profit business world. The Idaho office was in good shape when I inherited it and Felix made certain I wouldn't do much to ruin it. He was a marvelous mentor. His mantra was "Keep it simple, underpromise, and overdeliver"—a philosophy I adopted as my own and have never wavered from since.

Felix's office was in Seattle but every week I would receive memos from him on these green sheets of paper he liked to use with specific, detailed instructions about what I should be doing and when. These memos came in the mail, a process in great vogue at the time that involved someone putting a message in an envelope, depositing it in a mailbox, and the recipient on the other end picking it up in another mailbox. It usually took about three days to get a message from Seattle to Boise in this manner. Sounds primitive, I know, but it worked and it was remarkably effective.

One of Felix's mandates was that I needed to visit each chapter in the state every six months, at least. Armed with my marching orders, and with the longtime office secretary, Wanda Mulder, running the one-room office in Boise and keeping me on the straight and narrow, I got busy traveling the length and width of the aptly named Gem State. If Idaho doesn't have the finest—and mostly undiscovered— scenery, with the most variety, of any state in the country, I would like to argue the point. Driving in and of itself gave me time to think and get creative. From Nampa to West Yellowstone, from Montpelier to

McCall, I traveled through rich farmland, magnificent forests, spectacular rivers and gorges, wildlife of all description. They should charge money for the drive from Ketchum to Stanley, or Challis to Salmon, or Boise to McCall, or when you cross the bridge into Twin Falls, come around the corner, and see the falls. Take your pick, really. (Unless there's a blizzard; then all bets are off).

But trumping it all was the spirit of volunteerism I discovered. In towns and cities all over Idaho, I saw people who were the very embodiment of "doing it for the right reason." Good, selfless people determined to improve their community's quality of life.

To this point in my life I'd had little to no exposure to charity work. I'd see a panhandler on the street and most of the time walk right on by. It wasn't that I didn't have empathy. I certainly knew what it was to be poor. I grew up in a house without indoor plumbing. My father lived paycheck to paycheck and too often paycheck to no paycheck. It was, for all that, a wonderful life.

The closest I'd come to working in any kind of enterprise that looked out for others was when I was thirteen years old in Iowa and got a part time weekend job working for the Bureau of Indian Affairs. One weekend I was part of a crew that delivered brand new washers and dryers to the Winnebago Indian Reservation just south of Sioux City across the border in Nebraska. We dropped the appliances at the homes of the Indians living on the reservation, courtesy of the Interior Department, Bureau of Indian Affairs. However, the government had overlooked one minor detail. None of those homes had electricity!

All those washers and dryers just sat in the front yards. For all I know, they're still sitting there.

So I had no real reference point in the world of effective community organizing; and virtually no exposure to altruism— the desire, as defined in the dictionary, "to act out of concern for another's well-being, not because you are obligated to, but because you feel like helping."

Idaho, I soon realized, was full of altruism. Tom Abbott, my predecessor, had left the state well organized and productive.

I first met the chapter chairs in each county; people who had "how can I help?" written into their DNA, full of energy, good will, and a healthy dose of competitive spirit.

There was Sherrie Hansen of Blackfoot. Sherrie was a young mother of three. Her husband was a schoolteacher. She was president of the Jaycee-ettes, the female arm (back in more sexist times) of the Jaycees, the service group affiliated with the U.S. Junior Chamber of Commerce. She had organized the most successful walkathon in the state, using her husband's influence to get her into the schools. She had as much energy and determination as a Texas high school football coach. Maybe more. When Sherrie walked in the room, everybody listened.

There were Bob and Sandy Becker of Twin Falls—a husband-wife team. He was president of the Jaycees, she was president of the Jaycee-ettes. They didn't have any children yet. They could have focused solely on themselves and building up their material possessions. Instead, they taught me how to organize a community—how to take the lead in providing service and giving something back. They wanted to make a difference.

There was Arnold Hagmann, a cop in Boise. Arnold and I became great friends. We did a Christmas program where for a fifty-dollar donation you could have a Boise police officer come to your home and bring Santa Claus with him to visit with your kids. We quickly realized that the kids were far more enamored with the police officer than they were with Santa.

There were Imogene Carrico and Linda Hagmann and Larry Cash and hundreds more just like them, people whose only motivation was to make the world a better place. They were givers, not takers; doers, not watchers. They weren't participating because they had to or were supposed to, but because they wanted to and they could. Doctors and plumbers and lawyers and salespeople and homemakers and welders and plumbers and cops and teachers and bankers and more than one or two potato farmers. Rich people, poor people, everything in between. It was all very eye-opening to me, this way of life, this volunteerism, this selflessness. I quickly realized that no one was working for me; I was working for them. Without the non-paid volunteers, I didn't have a job. I didn't stand a chance. With them, I not only had a job, but a constant source of inspiration and motivation.

It didn't hurt that the March of Dimes was such an easy sell. The cause was to fight and eliminate birth defects. Who could argue with that? As an organization, the March of Dimes had been around since 1938, when President Franklin D. Roosevelt, during his second term in the White House, founded a private charity called the National Foundation for Infantile Paralysis, or NFIP. The goal of the NFIP was to find a cure for polio, the viral infection that paralyzed or killed over half a million people in the world every year. A highly contagious disease that was virtually unknown prior to the twentieth century, from 1900 on polio epidemics had been flaring up with regularity in one section after another in the United States. Of course for FDR, who had been diagnosed with polio as a young man and relegated to a wheelchair much of his adult life, the cause was intensely personal.

The country was quick to rally behind the president's emotional call to action. The NFIP's inaugural fundraising campaign was centered around FDR's birthday, calling for people to send a letter to the White House with a dime inside. In no time, the White House mail room was inundated. During a single day, on January 30, 1938, the president's birthday, between forty and fifty thousand letters arrived. "A silver tide," it was called. In all, $85,000 was raised by this single "March of Dimes" campaign event. By year's end, the tally was $1.8 million—all this during the Great Depression, mind you.

The NFIP approach single-handedly changed the way charitable funds were raised. Instead of soliciting large donations from a few wealthy individuals, small donations were solicited from millions of ordinary wage-earning Americans. A wide variety of fundraising campaigns were developed and implemented by Basil O'Connor, FDR's friend and the foundation's first president. At Christmas time, booths were set up on street corners where people could drop in dimes. O'Connor organized the country into local chapters—the forerunner of the structure I inherited in Idaho—to oversee the collection and proper dispersal of the donations. In this manner, the organization raised vast sums of money that funded intense research to provide care for polio patients and find a cure—some $233 million by 1955 ($2.1 billion in 2019 dollars). That's the year the vaccine successfully developed by Dr. Jonas Salk, thanks to NFIP funding, was introduced to the public and millions upon millions began getting immunized. Polio hadn't been cured, but the Salk Vaccine effectively wiped out polio as an epidemic.

Americans became so enamored of the power of the dime that in 1946, a year after his death, Franklin D. Roosevelt was honored by having his likeness put on the dime. (Replacing the profile of Winged Liberty).

That was the March of Dimes legacy.

In 1958, with virtually every child in the country immunized against polio, the NFIP dropped "Infantile Paralysis" from its name and became the National Foundation. Its new focus: birth defects. Technically, that was the organization I joined in 1973, although by then everyone referred to it as the March of Dimes. (In 1976 the name was officially changed to the March of Dimes Birth Defects Foundation. In 2007 it became simply the March of Dimes Foundation).

When I got to Idaho, the March of Dimes brand—although no one used the term "brand" back then—was as strong as it had ever been. Just a few years earlier, the organization had helped support and fund the successful development of a vaccine for Rubella, or German measles, a known cause of birth defects that included blindness, deafness, and mental retardation.

My job was to keep the brand rolling. I'd go from county to county helping the chapters plan and organize fundraisers. The

March of Dimes had a wealth of impressive marketing materials to help generate interest. At national headquarters in New York, a filmmaker named Ed Franck produced beautiful, incredible motivational films. When I'd go to a Jaycee meeting or a Kiwanis club or a school I'd show these films. One of the most popular was one that showed the birth of a baby. You could count on a tear or two while that one was playing. Which is why I was so surprised when everyone in the room exploded into laughter when I was showing the film to a group in Idaho Falls.

I'd lugged my big reel-to-reel projector in from the car and set it up in the back of the conference room at the Ramada Inn. About seventy Jaycees and Jaycee-ettes were in attendance. It was a cold winter evening outside. Inside it was warm and toasty and they all sat there, ready and waiting to be motivated. I turned on the projector and started the film. As soon as it began I could see I had neglected to rewind the film the last time I showed it. It was at the end instead of the beginning. With my back to the screen, I flipped the lever on the projector to rewind the film. A moment later, the whole room was in an uproar. I turned around and saw what had everyone laughing so hard: they were watching the birth of the baby backwards. Yup... you got it... that little squirt just popped right back up in there.

We did a Mothers March every year. That's where moms, not unlike an encyclopedia or vacuum salesperson, would go door to door asking for donations. It was Mothers Marches that had raised considerable funding for the polio vaccine. Our most successful fundraisers were the Walkathons. We did those every year. Volunteers, mostly kids, would commit to walk twenty miles on a designated route and collect per-mile pledges from donors. In Blackfoot, Sherrie Hansen taught me a lot about organizing the community. She planned, organized and delivered the number one Walkathon in the state, with around six hundred walkers who had secured donations of over $17,000. Sherrie offered a variety of prizes to walkers excelling in various categories. She was able to recruit more walkers with those incentives. She coordinated an assembly at the local middle school and gave away bicycles and other prizes that had been donated by local merchants to walkers who raised the most money. Sherrie was truly "all in."

When the other chapters around the state saw what Sherrie was doing they picked up their game. The state's biggest chapter in Boise doubled their results the next year. That next year I secured the donation of a new car from a local car dealer as a first prize. The parents were suddenly incentivized to support their kids in the fundraiser.

We'd keep a running tally of who raised what and present awards every year to the most productive chapters. In fundraising, as in football, competition is a wonderful thing. It brings out the best in people. We had the number one per capita walkathon in the country.

. . . .

The final component I became acquainted with in this new world I'd become a part of was the medical community: another area I had little familiarity with, and certainly no expertise in. I'd majored in history and political science. I played football. I worked construction jobs to pay for college. Doctors, nurses, hospital administrators, emergency rooms, diseases, vaccines, birth defects—it was all foreign territory to me. I didn't understand the terrain. I didn't speak the language.

As with the volunteers who ran the chapters and signed up for the fundraisers, I grew to deeply appreciate the professionalism and commitment of the pediatric healthcare providers.

I became friends with Henrietta Andress, the head nurse for the Newborn Intensive Care Unit at St. Luke's Hospital in Boise. She insisted that I rock a preemie in my arms. It wasn't something I ever would have done on my own. But Henrietta was persistent. She set up a schedule for every member on the March of Dimes Board to sit in a rocking chair in the NICU and have a hands-on, eyeball-to-eyeball experience with a preemie you could almost fit in one hand. She knew how critical it was to their growth and development for those newborns to be touched, and how critical it was for people like me and others involved in the cause to have that personal connection and understand on the most basic level that their welfare was in our hands.

I was a nervous wreck the first time. It was more *don't hurt this baby* that ran through my mind than anything else. They are so tiny and they're usually hooked up to tubes and wires, so it's an intense experience when you're not used to it. But my heart just melted. I've always been emotional, so I'm easily moved, but I think a statue would feel something looking down at a little baby that you know is fighting its mightiest to live. (For the next thirty-plus years, until I retired, whenever I was traveling on the job and could find the time, I would go to the children's hospital and find the NICU and rock babies; Henrietta really started something).

In Idaho I was introduced to my first pediatricians. It didn't take long before I realized that these doctors who have chosen to specialize in child care are very special people. They don't make the most money. They don't drive the flashiest cars. They aren't brain surgeons, they're not plastic surgeons. They don't have runaway egos, they're not concerned with who gets the credit. What they do is **put the best interests of kids first**. That's their priority. It's all about the kids, period. I was so impressed by that. I wondered if this was something unique to Idaho; as time went on, I would come to find out it's something unique to pediatricians.

Working collaboratively, we were able to make significant strides in providing healthcare for newborns. At St. Luke's, Henrietta Andress led the effort to bring in a full time neonatologist. (A neonatologist is a pediatrician who specializes in medical care of newborn infants, especially those that are ill or premature). Idaho had never had a neonatologist. That changed when every chapter in the state pooled their fundraising together and come up with enough money—$200,000—to get the national March of Dimes office to award a grant of $150,000-a-year for the next five years. With those funds, St. Luke's was able to recruit a young, highly regarded neonatologist in Dallas, Dr. Tom Wells, to move to Boise and set up an essential Level One Newborn Intensive Care Unit at the hospital. After watching the friendly but intense competition between the chapters, I was gratified they all agreed to collaborate. It truly was a statewide effort. And a huge win for Idaho's newborns. It meant that babies born in local community hospitals in need of urgent care would now be transported to Boise for the best care possible.

A year after that, we won another national March of Dimes grant to start Idaho's first statewide perinatal program. (Perinatal refers to the period of time from three months before a child is born to a month after). It was a shot in the dark, but we applied for it and got that too!—another $150,000-a-year for five years. Dr. Wells at St. Luke's worked with Dr. Zsolt Koppanyi, chief of the Idaho Bureau of Child Health, and Dr. Larry Jung, director of the University of Utah's NICU in Salt Lake City, to develop a program that delivered ongoing education to doctors and nurses working in Idaho hospitals, as well as establishing protocols for transporting newborns in need of critical care in Idaho to either Boise or Salt Lake City.

We were also able to place fetal monitors in hospitals throughout Idaho, allowing nurses and doctors to better assess the pulse rate and rhythm of the heart of a fetus. Last but not least, we brought in the state's first pediatric cardiologist, Dr. Dale Henken, who joined Dr. Wells at St. Luke's.

The inertia from all this progress was nearly palpable. As the sports announcers would say, we had momentum on our side. Every year, fundraising climbed. In 1973, the year I arrived, the state had raised $400,000 for the March of Dimes. By 1977 we were raising over $1 million annually. With the help of wonderful people like Sherrie Hansen and Bob and Sandy Becker and Arnold Hagmann and Imogene Carrico and Henrietta Andress and Mike King, who managed the MiniDome in Pocatello and never said no to a single request, and great TV and radio station managers like Rod Arquette at KFXD Radio in Meridian and Craig Clyde at Boise's KBOI TV, Idaho became the Number One per capita fundraising state for the March of Dimes. We were second to none!

Then one afternoon the phone rang. Glenn Thomas, the March of Dimes regional director in Denver, was on the line, Felix's counterpart. The Utah chapter was part of his region. Utah's longtime director, Bruce Hanks, a legend in March of Dimes circles who had led the chapter for the past twenty-eight years, was retiring. Would I be interested in interviewing for the position?

The next week I found myself at Willow Creek Country Club south of Salt Lake City. Thomas had arranged a golf game so we could get acquainted. Elmer Smith, who was Chairman of the Board of the Utah Chapter of the March of Dimes, joined us.

I was not a golfer. When we were finished playing, I remember Thomas saying, "Well, I can tell you're probably pretty dedicated to your work because you sure haven't been spending your time golfing."

Anyway, they offered me the job, and I accepted.

I drove back to Boise with conflicting emotions. Four and a half years in Idaho had changed me. I had come for a filler job, just something to do on my way to teaching history and coaching football. Instead, I became immersed in a world of caring people helping protect our most precious resource: babies. Every day was challenging, exciting, fun. I loved the competition, I loved the organizing, I loved connecting the dots to help make a whole bigger than the sum of the parts. Work was not a chore. I had found something I loved to do. I came to Idaho needing a paycheck; I was leaving with a career.

It felt good to depart on a high note. I was beyond flattered by the tribute from Dr. Zsolt Koppanyi, chief of the Idaho Bureau of Child Health, when he recommended me for the new job in Utah, chronicling the contributions we had made. In a letter to

Elmer Smith, chapter chairman of the Utah March of Dimes, Dr. Koppyani wrote:

Dear Mr. Smith:

It is my understanding that Mr. Milton Shannon of Boise is applying for a position with your organization.

With pleasure, I recommend Mr. Shannon for your consideration. I am certain you are aware of the fundraising success the Ada-Boise Chapter has had under Mr. Shannon's leadership. In addition, however, I wish to point out some of the significant program developments with which Mr. Shannon has been associated here.

"Mick" was largely responsible for the awarding of a multi-year MOD grant to our Bureau for initial development of Genetic Counselling clinic services in Idaho. The program is now a regular feature of our agency and, following the demonstration period is now supported with state and federal funds.

Another area of Mr. Shannon's involvement relates to the improvement of peri-natal care services in Idaho. Through the Chapter's intervention, St. Luke's Hospital of Boise has been able to upgrade its newborn care facilities so that it functions as a regional resource for high-risk infants. "Mick" has much to do with attracting the first neonatologist to the area with MOD Support Grants. Also, he has taken an active role in planning and carrying out various training programs for professionals involved in perinatal care services

Mr. Shannon has coordinated MOD activities effectively with other state and private agencies and this is a most important aspect in a state such as ours with limited resources.

While we would regret losing this individual to Idaho, we appreciate that other opportunities would be available to him. We believe you would find him to be an effective administrator and a strong advocate for improving services to mothers and children.

Sincerely,

Zsolt Koppanyi, M.D., M.P.H., F.A.A.P.
Chief, Bureau of Child Health

And this from Dr. Dale Henken, the first pediatric cardiologist in Idaho:

Dear Mr. Smith:

It is my distinct pleasure to recommend to you Mr. Milton (Mick) P. Shannon, Director of the March of Dimes for the state of Idaho. I have worked closely with Mr. Shannon over the past year in my capacity as the Director of the Idaho State Perinatal Project and currently as the Medical Advisory Chairman of the Boise-Ada County Chapter of the March of Dimes.

Mr. Shannon was an essential architect in the design of our statewide perinatal project. He worked diligently with Dr. Thomas Wells, our first Perinatal Project Director, getting the grant accepted by the National Foundation.

In nearly single handed fashion he sold the project to the various, often conflicting, agencies concerned with perinatal care in our state and tenaciously supported the project during periods of waning enthusiasm.

His grasp of the need for and means to improve perinatal care, the stated purpose of the March of Dimes, is phenomenal for a person without extensive medical training. He has a unique ability as a salesperson and speaks persuasively to an audience. He combines competence with unflagging enthusiasm. However, he also listens well to advice from others and is careful to incorporate the ideas of others in his decisions. He delegates responsibllity well but remains available for guidance.

I rarely have the opportunity to write about someone of his ability and I can, without reservation, recommend him to you.

Sincerely,

Dale P. Henken, M.D., MCD-MAC

I tied up the loose ends in Boise and headed off in the direction of Utah: back to where we'd come from. 270,000 miles later, I felt good about what me and that little orange Toyota had done, even as the floorboard had worn out underneath the driver's seat and I watched the highway pass beneath my feet.

1980 March of Dimes Telethon—Mick with Fred Ferre and Sherry Shelton

CHAPTER THREE

....

Back to the Future

Everything about Utah was on a larger scale: more people, more volunteers, larger county organizations, bigger staff (and for me, a bigger salary). The Board of Trustees played a very extensive role. In Idaho I'd reported to a Board, but most everything I asked for was approved without much discussion. In Utah, the Board was in control, overseeing an organization that included, in addition to the headquarters office in Salt Lake City, branch offices in Ogden in the north end of the state and Provo in the south. My job as executive director was limited to the Salt Lake Chapter. I wouldn't be traveling nearly as much. I replaced the little orange Toyota with a four-year-old light blue Ford Galaxie I bought from my father-in-law.

The chapter was in terrific shape. Over his long tenure, Bruce Hanks, a man whose more than two decades of leadership with the March Of Dimes dated back to before polio was conquered, had grown Utah into a model of efficiency, one of the best-run and top-producing chapters in the country. Utah perennially ranked first, second or third in the country in per capita giving (in 1977 it was second only to Idaho). The March of Dimes had a local reputation as a charity that could be counted on and trusted. I was inheriting a first-rate organization. I was excited to collaborate with, and learn from, the Salt Lake Chapter Board of Trustees.

I was comfortable with the move. I knew the territory. Idaho was right next door. I'd gone to school in Utah; I was a loyal BYU graduate, I was a member of the majority religion. It felt like I was coming back home.

It helped that I already knew many of the leaders involved in children's health care in Utah, in particular Dr. Larry Jung at the University of Utah who had been so supportive in helping us set up the NICU at St. Luke's in Boise, and the Idaho perinatal program. In 1968, Dr. Jung had established the first NICU in the Intermountain West at the University of Utah Medical Center; in 1978, right after I arrived, he followed that up by setting up the NICU at Primary Children's Medical Center. Dr. Jung's personal story was typical of many who become passionate about newborn care. He was majoring in forestry at college when a child of his was born with cerebral palsy. Seeing firsthand how important early detection of birth defects can be, he switched his major to medicine, became a pediatrician, and dedicated his life to looking out for kids starting life with medical hurdles to overcome. Dr. Jung embodied everything that was right about being a pediatrician and caring for newborns.

A great example of the cooperation between the University of Utah NICU and the Idaho perinatal program took place soon after I arrived in Utah. Donnie Skaggs, a Board member for the Utah March of Dimes, had an interesting proposal. He asked for a meeting with Dr. Jung at the University of Utah. Donnie wanted to film the transport of a critically ill patient from a local hospital to the University of Utah. We all thought it would be a great story representing how the March of Dimes and the various health institutions worked together. Donnie had access to a Lear jet through the Skaggs corporation, the regional drugstore chain his family had founded. The plan was to identify a transport and put everything in motion to document that process from beginning to end. We would pre-tape the helicopter taking the transport team to the airport and the transport team boarding the fixed wing aircraft for the flight to the referring hospital. Then all we had to do was wait for the phone to ring with the ideal situation to execute our plan. Not every transport would work. We waited until the call came in that fit our criteria and the plan was put in motion.

The patient was a four-day-old newborn in Twin Falls, Idaho, with a major heart defect. We filmed the fixed wing transport aircraft taking off from Salt Lake. Then we boarded the Lear jet, quickly taking off for Twin Falls. We were able to shoot air to air video of the transport team's plane and land in Twin Falls far ahead of the transport plane. We filmed the landing and the team's transfer to the ambulance to go to the hospital to prepare the baby for transport. Then we simply reversed the process, filming the baby boarding the aircraft, the aircraft taking off, air to air on the return, landing in Salt Lake, boarding the helicopter from the airport to the hospital. On these kinds of transports, the parents of the infant would have to drive to Salt Lake. As we were leaving Twin Falls, it occurred to us that this was a unique opportunity for the mother to join us and be there when her baby arrived in Salt Lake. The father could follow later with whatever support was needed. The mother was greatly relieved at the opportunity. After landing in Salt Lake, I was able to drive the mother to the University of Utah to be there when her baby arrived. The next morning, as Donnie and I were thanking Larry for setting this opportunity up, learning the baby was going to undergo open heart surgery, Donnie pushed the envelope. He asked Larry, "What if we could film the open heart surgery?" Larry said, "I can't remember that ever being done. Let me meet with the surgeons." They all thought the photography equipment could be wrapped in a sterile environment. And bingo! We have film of that baby's heart beating between the two fingers of the surgeon. That film became one of the most powerful videos ever produced for the national March of Dimes.

It was a remarkable group of people I joined at the Utah chapter. There was nothing passive about the way they went about things. It started at the top. The Board of Trustees was very much hands-on. Fred Ferre, Sherry Shelton, Alan Hague, Stan Brewer, Norm Chesler, Elmer Smith, Phil Arlt—I'll never forget their passion and drive. They didn't just direct, they *did*. When I arrived, they threw their arms around me, figuratively and literally. They wanted the chapter to continue to succeed. They wanted me to succeed. It had a profound effect on me. I was the youngest person in the room. I watched and learned.

Fred and Sherry really took me under their wing. Fred was a successful local businessman, owner and operator of F.G. Ferre & Sons Auto Parts, with locations around the Salt Lake Valley. Sherry was a socialite. Her husband was a banker. She lived high on the east bench overlooking Salt Lake. She was wealthy and could spend her time as she pleased. Like Fred, she chose to spend a sizeable portion of it helping the March of Dimes.

The Utah chapter had many of the same programs as Idaho, including the Mothers March and the Walkathon, along with several of its own. Bruce's team had partnered with an interior designer, Bob Dunfield, to create and promote the largest haunted house fundraising activity in the country, known to locals as The Old Mill Haunted House. This event alone raised over $300,000 yearly.

The chapter also had something else: its very own telethon.

A telethon, as the name suggests, combines television with a marathon of programming to raise funds for a cause. For years, the Jerry Lewis MDA Labor Day Telethon had been the model for this brand of fundraising: broadcasting around the clock every Labor Day weekend to raise money for the Muscular Dystrophy Association. That was a national event, carried by hundreds of television stations from coast to coast. The Utah March of Dimes telethon, on the other hand, was strictly a local event, a replication of sorts of what Jerry Lewis did, but on a smaller scale, broadcast by one station: the local CBS affiliate (at the time) in Salt Lake City, KSL-TV.

When I arrived in Utah, only weeks remained until the next telethon. That's where all the focus was. I quickly learned two things: One was how much I didn't know about putting on a telethon. The second was how much the people I'd just joined did.

The show aired every year in January for twenty-one straight hours from Saturday night to Sunday afternoon, with KSL's on-air talent serving as the show's hosts and local celebrities and entertainers providing the programming content. Dozens of volunteers sat at phone banks set up on the stage to accept donations called in by viewers. Corporate sponsors generated about half the income. That more than covered the overhead operating costs because KSL donated the twenty-one hours of air time. That was a huge savings. If the chapter had to pay for air time, there probably wouldn't have been a telethon. On top of that, KSL provided producers and other technicians from its staff free of charge. The relationship between the Utah chapter and KSL was the glue that held it all together and made the telethon such a perennial success. It was obvious how much positive nurturing had taken place over the years. I could tell these people really liked and respected each other.

I met Al Henderson and Mike Mischler, guys about my age who worked full time for KSL and were the main producers of the telethon. Shortly after we'd been introduced, I shared with them some of my ideas for the show. First they just stared at me, then they started laughing, then they went about their business. I cracked them up. Looking back, I realize it was a little like telling LeBron James how to run the floor. They were absolute masters at what they did. I might have taken offense— matter of fact, I seem to remember I *did* take offense—at them laughing at my brainstorms, until I watched them in action.

I mainly tried to stay out of the way during my first experience with the telethon in January of 1978. The production was staged at the Special Events Center at the University of Utah. I answered phones along with the rest of the staff and volunteers and watched a parade of local celebrities and corporate donors come on the show to be interviewed by local media personalities. There was a nice eclectic variety of entertainment, including a handful of Hollywood luminaries with local ties—an impressive lineup for a local show. One of the acts was a man from Vernal, Utah, who had drawn a comical face on his rather robust belly and contorted his midsection in time to a song he proceeded to sing. See the dancing belly once and you'll never forget it. To borrow from Al Michaels, "You can't make this stuff up."

The telethon was a tremendous energizer, spilling over into every other fundraiser we did. In spring we always held the Walk America Walkathon. I was constantly trying to come up with creative ways to get more participation, especially from young people, who tended to make up most of the walkers. My thinking was that we should bring in a big name celebrity that teenagers would flock to the event to see. On the theory if you're going to dream, you might as well dream big, my goal was to get the hottest new teen heartthrob in show business.

Mick with the old guy, Joe Lake

....

CHAPTER FOUR

Smartest Thing I Ever Did

If I had any chance of getting the hottest new teen heartthrob in show business, I knew the man I had to see: Joe Lake.

Joe was a March of Dimes volunteer who helped provide entertainment for the annual telethon. I didn't know him well, but as I sat back and watched the people behind the scenes who made things happen, I could see that here was a man with a unique talent to definitely make things happen.

Joe had skills I didn't have. He had skills most people don't have. I knew how to manage an organization, balance the budget, dream up programs, plot strategies, foster competition. Those were strengths. I could also tend to be laser focused and project oriented, my attention focused more on the goal than on the people achieving it. Joe wasn't like that. Joe was a people person; a networker; a hustler; a diplomat. I liked people, but I was a little socially awkward. A few years later, after CMN was up and running, I was having lunch with a friend and sponsor in Los Angeles. "You know," he said. "You are lucky you have Joe Lake." I asked him why. He said, "Because you're not that likeable." He was teasing me and we laughed, but the best jokes always contain a grain of truth.

Joe was likeable. He was gregarious; a natural-born salesman, the kind who could sell the proverbial ice to Eskimo.

Our backgrounds, like our personalities, couldn't have been much different. His life was as conventional as mine was unconventional. Raised in Salt Lake City in a middle-class family, Joe Lake grew up in a house on the east side of the valley that definitely had indoor plumbing. He went on a two-year Mormon mission to Scotland and Ireland after high school and attended the University of Utah, where he earned a bachelor's degree in business management. Joe's dad worked at an insurance agency, where Joe worked too, both during and after graduating college. It was anticipated he would eventually take the business over.

But selling life insurance at a desk, nine to five, didn't cut it for Joe Lake. It was too confining, too structured. He bored easily. When the agent who worked at the desk next to his, Jake Garn, decided he wanted to run for mayor of Salt Lake City, Joe volunteered to work on his campaign. Garn won and politics became Joe's avocation. He joined the national Young Republicans and worked on a congressional campaign for Sherm Lloyd and then on Jake Garn's senatorial campaign when he ran for the United States Senate two years after being elected mayor. Garn, and Joe, won that one too.

Joe was a networker before people started calling people like him networkers. He was drawn to people, that was the bottom line. He liked getting to know them; liked endearing himself to them; liked helping them out and letting them help him out. "The most important word in the English language is relationships," he'd always say. "And relationships are different than acquaintances."

Relationships had value. Relationships were a two-way street. Relationships made the world go round. Relationships got things done.

As he continued selling insurance, Joe stayed active in politics, including doing work as a volunteer advance man for Richard Nixon—well before the Watergate years. But he was restless just selling insurance, so when a business partner asked him for his help in setting up a new advertising and public relations agency, he was all in.

The Lake and Shannon Kids

For the ad company's first Christmas party, it fell to Joe to find the entertainment. He knew three young men from Salt Lake who had formed a band called Sunshade 'n Rain and were looking for places to play. Joe invited them to sing at the party. Everyone was stunned at how good they were. Joe asked the trio what they charged. They said fifteen dollars—five dollars apiece. (Bear in mind, this was in the 1960s, but still). Joe paid them their fee, and added another five dollars for a tape they were selling, and they went on their way. But it nagged at him that these musicians with all that talent weren't getting anything close to what they were worth. After a few weeks he called them and asked who represented them. Nobody, they said. They represented themselves.

"How would you like me to represent you?" he asked, and that is how Joe Lake got into the entertainment business.

Soon enough, Sunshade 'n Rain, now under the new management of Joe Lake, was playing in Reno, Las Vegas, New Orleans, and elsewhere in the showroom circuit around the country—for a lot more than fifteen dollars. They opened for headliners like Bill Cosby and Johnny Mathis and the 5th Dimension, and thanks to their new, energetic agent, negotiated a record deal. There's no telling how far Sunshade 'n Rain might have gone, but the boys in the band all got married and decided to concentrate more on family life and less on travel. But Joe was on his way, making connections and cementing relationships here, there, and everywhere. He quit selling insurance entirely and put the ad/pr thing on the back burner. He was in show biz.

His reputation soon began preceding him. A case in point was the Utah chapter of the March of Dimes. Bruce Hanks, my predecessor as executive director, had a brother named Duff Hanks who was a general authority with the LDS Church. One day Joe Lake got a call from Duff Hanks, a family friend and longtime client of Joe's father in the insurance business. Duff had heard about Joe's work with Sunshade 'n Rain and was calling on behalf of his brother. He asked Joe if he would please give Bruce a call. The March of Dimes put on a telethon every January and Bruce was hoping Joe might help bring Sunshade 'n Rain and maybe some other entertainers on the show.

The odd thing was, when I arrived in Utah, Joe's services weren't being used to any large extent on the telethon. He helped book a few acts for the show, including Sunshade 'n Rain. But Sherry Shelton was on the Board, was well connected socially, knew a number of mid-level celebrities herself, and she took a proprietary interest in handling the entertainment and guests. That was her area and she guarded it zealously.

Still, from my vantage point behind the scenes, it wasn't hard to see Joe's abilities. When he said he could make something happen, it happened. Time and again I watched him work his networking magic.

So in the afterglow of another successful telethon in 1980, Joe Lake was the first person I thought of when I set out to find a big name for our next Walk America walkathon.

The celebrity I set my sights on—the hottest new teen heartthrob in America—was John Schneider.

John Schneider with RJ Shannon and Marci Lake

....

CHAPTER FIVE

Biggest Heart A Man Ever Had

John Schneider was the breakout star of the most popular show on television, *The Dukes of Hazzard*. He played Beauregard "Bo" Duke, a good 'ol Georgia country boy who gets into all sorts of scrapes and shenanigans with his cousin Luke (played by Tom Wopat) and their beautiful cousin Daisy (played by Catharine Bach)—most of the time while running from the law in their souped-up Dodge Charger, the *General Lee*. Waylon Jennings sang the show's theme song, *Good Ol' Boys*, which was also a big hit.

John Schneider was a chiseled six-foot-three, two hundred pounds, blond-haired, blue-eyed, twenty years old, with looks that were a cross between Robert Redford and Brad Pitt. He was on the cover of every teenage magazine of the day. Merchandisers were selling millions of his dolls, toy replicas of the *General Lee*, and other Dukes gear. In 1980 there was no more popular young entertainer out there.

"What are the chances we could get in touch with John Schneider?" I asked Joe.

Instead of looking at me like I'd lost my mind, he said, "Let me do some digging."

Joe subscribed to a book that listed contact information for people in the entertainment industry: actors, singers, producers, agents, and so forth. He turned to the page with John Schneider's contacts. His agent was a man named Mike Gursey.

Joe, it so happened, knew Mike Gursey. They'd worked on bookings for Sunshade 'n Rain when Gursey was with the William Morris Agency, before he branched out on his own to become an independent agent.

Joe called Mike. Mike answered. Because they knew each other, Mike didn't hang up.

In checking the dates for the walkathon, it turned out we were in luck. The young TV star was available at that time. He had an appearance fee, Mike informed Joe: $5,000 for the day.

We'd never paid anyone, but getting the No. 1 teen heartthrob in the nation seemed like a good place to start.

I talked to KSL about participating in the event by flying John Schneider to various Walkathon locations around the state in the station's helicopter, Chopper Five. KSL readily agreed. *The Dukes of Hazzard* was a CBS show that ran on KSL. The publicity from having the star in Utah certainly wouldn't hurt ratings. Beyond that, KSL was the kind of business that did things for no other reason than to help the community.

In advance of Schneider's appearance, we advertised heavily on billboards, on public service radio and TV spots, and papered the schools with posters.

To give John company, I invited a young football player at BYU, quarterback Jim McMahon, to join us. Since returning to Utah, I'd joined the Cougar Club, BYU's booster group, and hadn't missed a game. I'd gotten to know McMahon while watching BYU's practices, something I did whenever I could find the time—I suppose you could call football my therapy. Before he was through Jim McMahon would rewrite huge portions of the record book—at BYU and the entire NCAA—and then go on to the NFL and win a Super Bowl with the Chicago Bears. But in the spring of 1980 he was an unknown college kid with time on his hands. He said sure, he'd come along.

We loaded up the helicopter and flew to nine different walkathon locations that day, from one end of the state to the other. We'd printed ahead of time nine thousand autographed photographs of John. We should have printed more. Twelve thousand-plus kids participated in the Walkathons, a thirty percent increase over the year before, the majority of them shrieking teenage girls. We ended up raising $310,000, setting a local March of Dimes Walkathon record.

Mick, John Schneider, and Joe

At the end of the day, we drove John Schneider and Mike Gursey back to the Salt Lake airport for their return flight to Los Angeles. At the gate, Joe Lake handed a check for $5,000 to Mike Gursey. John's appearance fee. Mike in turn handed the check to John.

John took the check, looked at it, turned it over, endorsed it, and handed it right back to Joe.

"This was for charity, wasn't it?" is all he said. Then he got on the plane. This young man was mature beyond his years; he had been raised right. Character and reputation were everything with him.

News of our Walkathon success spread quickly through the March of Dimes universe. In one day, we had conducted the most successful Walk America in the charity's history. Nobody could believe we got Bo Duke to participate. Nobody could believe the money we generated. Soon, the national office was on the line. Would John Schneider consider being the national Walk America chairman for the organization? Would Bo Duke become the face of the March of Dimes?

Again, Joe Lake talked to Mike Gursey who talked to John Schneider. Again, John said yes. National wanted pictures of him with children for promotional purposes. John returned to Utah and posed for a photo shoot with my ten-year-old son RJ and Joe's ten-year-old daughter Marci. Soon, RJ's and Marci's faces—along with John Schneider's—were on two thousand billboards all across the country and literally millions of 7-Eleven Slurpee cups.

The experience with John Schneider clearly demonstrated that something that was successful on a local level could be transformed into something even more successful on a national level. Several months later, when our 1981 telethon came along, John agreed to come back to Utah and be part of the entertainment lineup. We expanded to include Boise in the production, giving the ABC TV station KIVI fifteen minutes each hour to raise funds for the Idaho March of Dimes chapter. Boise was thrilled with the arrangement. The telethon got their fundraising for the year off to a great start.

In the wake of all this success, the thought kept racing around in my mind: What if we spread the wealth even farther? What if, instead of just the two markets I was familiar with in Utah and Idaho, we aired the telethon in multiple markets? And what if we were able to attract more celebrities the caliber and character of John Schneider to appear on the show and draw in an even bigger audience?

And what could it hurt to try?

I immediately started collaborating with others to gauge if they were as enthusiastic as I was to expand to multiple markets. I talked to members of the Utah March of Dimes Board; to our telethon producers Al Henderson and Mike Mischler; to their bosses at KSL, general manager Jay Lloyd and president Arch Madsen. After all, it was their telethon. KSL was a critical player. Our relationship with the television station, the perennial ratings leader in the Intermountain West, was valuable in so many ways. Their cooperation, along with their agreeing to donate their satellite uplink and satellite air time, was our biggest selling point.

To a person, everyone I talked to felt it made sense to move forward. The Board agreed to allocate $110,000 to provide a salary for Joe Lake and cover limited travel and other expenses to recruit additional chapters and television markets to participate in the 1982 telethon. Now, we needed to find out if anyone out there was as excited as we were.

Our first stop was John Schneider to see if he would agree to host the telethon.

John was in California so that's where Joe and I went. We rented an economy car, drove to Hollywood, checked into a cheap Howard Johnson's right off the 101 and shared a room. The next morning, we drove out to Encino to the home of TV star Lee Majors, where John was playing tennis with the *Six Million Dollar Man*. Mike Gursey represented both John and Lee and asked us to meet at Lee's house. We waited with Mike for the tennis game to finish.

John was more popular than ever. *The Dukes of Hazzard*, now entering its third season, remained solidly entrenched among the top-watched shows on television. As a singer, John had recorded his first album, *It's Now or Never*. The title track made it to No. 4 on the country music charts and No. 14 in popular music—a genuine crossover hit, pointing to John's appeal to all genres.

But there was no indication that fame and fortune had changed him in the slightest. He was the same man who'd thrown his appearance fee back at us two years earlier. Of course he wanted to be involved with an expanded telethon, he told us—as long as we didn't pay him anything.

Everything was falling into place as Joe and I steered back toward Utah. We had the commitment we needed from the Board, we had the facilities we needed from KSL, we had the talent. Now we needed to see if we could attract the person we envisioned as the perfect fit to host the show with John Schneider, an entertainer who stride for stride could match his star power, youth, enthusiasm, and spirit.

Joe Lake, Marie Osmond, and Mick

....

CHAPTER SIX

Classy, Compassionate Lady

The first time I encountered Marie Osmond had nothing to do with the children's charity she would later co-found.

Then again, I suppose it did.

In January of 1978, shortly after my return to Utah to run the March of Dimes chapter, I had taken my two daughters, seven-year-old Merrilee and five-year-old Amy, to a Saturday afternoon BYU-Arizona State basketball game. Following the game we stopped at Snelgrove's Ice Cream Parlor in the University Mall in Orem. We were the only ones in the store when Marie and a friend walked in. They sat at the counter directly across from our table. One of my girls said to the other, "She is as pretty as she was last night." The *Donny & Marie* show aired on Friday nights. We continued with our ice cream treat and Marie and her friend left.

A few minutes later, Marie and her friend returned. She had bought two little stuffed toys and autographed the ribbon around their necks. She had overheard the "pretty" comment and returned with the surprise for the girls. That is a kind, loving, compassionate person. She was eighteen.

Three years later, immediately after returning from our visit with John in California, Joe and I found ourselves sitting in Alan Osmond's house on Osmond Lane in Provo, Utah. At our request, Alan, the oldest of the singing Osmond Brothers, had called his sister Marie, who lived just up the street, to see if she could come by and meet us. Sure, she said, she'd be right over.

Marie Osmond was the ideal counterpart for John Schneider, a bona fide superstar in her own right. Her face was on magazine covers, her songs were on the radio, everyone knew her by her first name alone. She was no overnight sensation. Her star began to rise at an early age. She made her TV debut when she was just four, on *The Andy Williams Show,* and she was just thirteen when she recorded her first gold record, the crossover hit *Paper Roses.* Her popularity only expanded when she performed with Donny, her brother two years older. They started producing a string of hit singles and albums when she was fourteen and he was sixteen, beginning with *I'm Leaving It Up to You* and *Morning Side of the Mountain* in 1974. In 1975 they hosted a variety show on ABC that was so well received the network decided to turn it into a weekly program. *The Donny & Marie Show* made its debut in 1976. Donny and Marie Osmond, at eighteen and sixteen, were the youngest hosts of a weekly variety show in TV history. Dolls, figurines and other collectible was an offshoot of the show's personality and reach, just like that other hit Friday night show, *The Dukes of Hazzard.*

Marie and John had recently appeared together on a television special singing a duet on *The People's Choice Awards,* to rave reviews. They were the same age and had even briefly dated. Nothing serious had come of that but they remained good friends. Clearly, they had chemistry. Having them on stage together as co-hosts for our telethon would be a dream come true.

When Marie walked into her brother Alan's house she immediately put everyone at ease. Suzanne, Alan's wife, had made tuna fish sandwiches and as Marie helped herself to the sandwiches, Joe and I explained what we had in mind. We told Marie that John had already agreed to host the telethon and that we felt the two of them as co-hosts would be magnetic. We laid out our logistical plans to televise the show throughout the Intermountain West.

Then we started talking about what our charity was all about—helping kids—and we didn't need to say another word.

That was Marie's soft spot. Kids. Anything she could do to help children, in particular children battling health challenges, she wanted to be a part of. As soon as she heard that the cause was to help cure birth defects and help sick kids get better she didn't have to consult with anyone or take any time to think about it. Of course, we could count on her to participate, she said. Little could we realize at the time the portent of that commitment and promise. From the moment Marie sat at her brother's kitchen table and said "Yes" she was one hundred percent all-in.

The Osmond family dedicating a unit at St. Louis Children's Hospital, with CEO Alan Brass and Dairy Queen franchisee, Sam Temperato

....

CHAPTER SEVEN

The Osmonds

We weren't through asking the Osmonds for their assistance. We'd come to Alan and Suzanne's home to see if we could secure the use the Osmond Studios—again.

After years of holding the telethon at various sites in and around downtown Salt Lake City, the Osmond family—through a Joe Lake connection—had generously offered free use of the massive, state-of-the-art facility to televise the 1981 event.

Our hope was to be able to continue that relationship as we expanded the telethon's scope in 1982.

The Osmond Studios stood as a testament to the meteoric rise of the Osmonds, a family that thirty years earlier had started out with next to nothing in nearby Ogden, Utah, and proceeded to become a household name around the world.

The Osmond parents, George and Olive, had met during World War II at the army depot in Ogden where he was a sergeant and she was a secretary in the office pool.

They were married a year later, in 1944, and decided to settle down in Ogden (a city about eighty miles north of Orem) and start their family.

After that the kids came as if on a conveyor belt—nine children, eight of them boys, over the next eighteen years, spaced almost exactly two years apart except for the last one, Jimmy, who arrived four years after his sister Marie.

The first two sons, Virl and Tom, were born deaf, prompting their doctor, in one of life's rich ironies, to suggest to George and Olive that perhaps they shouldn't have any more children. Ignoring that advice, they had seven more, all with perfect hearing and a remarkable talent for singing. Over the course of the next thirty years, Alan, Wayne, Merrill, Jay, Donny, Marie, and Jimmy would go on to individually and collectively sell more than 100 million records. One of the first things they did with the proceeds from their earliest sales was fit Virl and Tom with hearing aids.

Alan, Wayne, Merrill, and Jay were the original Osmond Brothers—the act that first put the family name on the musical map. Their father, with no training as a marketer—he had a small farm in Ogden, worked at the post office and sold real estate in the early years to make ends meet—proved uncannily adept at promoting his boys. In 1959 he drove them to California, dressed in matching barbershop quartet outfits, and sent them onto Main Street at Disneyland, where they attracted the attention of The Dapper Dans, Disneyland's resident barbershop quartet.

The Dapper Dans asked the boys, aged twelve, ten, eight, and six, to sing them a song. When they did, a large crowd stopped to listen. By the time the Osmonds were headed home to Ogden, they'd been asked to return the next summer and perform as official Disneyland entertainers.

One thing kept leading to another. At Disneyland the next summer the brothers attracted the attention of Jay Williams, whose son Andy was starting a variety show on NBC. "Hey son, you should put these boys on your show," Jay urged. After auditioning the brothers, Andy agreed. In 1962 the Osmonds moved to Los Angeles. For the next nine years, until the *Andy Williams Show* left the air in 1971, the Osmond Brothers were a staple on the show. And not just them. Their little brothers Donny and Jimmy and their little sister Marie would all be introduced to the world on national television sitting on Andy Williams' lap.

Born just two years apart, Donny and Marie took the baton from their famous older brothers and kept running, taking the Osmond name to even greater heights. When ABC aired *The Donny & Marie Show* in 1976 the Osmond star was at its zenith. Royalties were rolling in. Hollywood was at their beck and call.

George and Olive had always dreamed of moving back to Utah. *The Donny & Marie Show* gave them their chance. They negotiated a deal with ABC that would allow them to film *The Donny & Marie Show* in Utah, providing they could find a studio capable of handling all the requirements.

Utah didn't have such a facility. So they built one.

Work was completed in 1976 on the massive Osmond Studios in Orem, located in the foothills of the Wasatch Mountains, just around the corner from the BYU campus. The airport in Salt Lake City was just fifty miles to the north. As soon as the studio was finished, all the Osmonds moved back to Utah and built homes on Osmond Lane overlooking the studio.

In every aspect, The Osmond Studios was cutting edge. From the wardrobe room to the lighting to the sound system to the massive stages, a finer production facility could not be found anywhere, in Hollywood or out. In addition to *The Donny & Marie Show*, numerous productions, from feature films to musical recordings to advertisements, started finding their way from Hollywood to Orem. Including our most recent March of Dimes telethon—and hopefully our next one.

Over Suzanne's lunch of milk, potato chips, and delicious tuna fish sandwiches—I can assure you Suzanne knows her way around a tuna fish sandwich—we were able to lay out our long-range goals for Alan. Alan arranged a second meeting to include brother Merrill. Having the use of the family's production facility would go a long way to reach those goals, we told them, and beyond that, our hope was to get the Osmond family more involved as celebrities and entertainers. Merrill caught the vision. For the 1981 telethon we had basically just been given the run of the place—an enormously generous offer in and of itself. But would the Osmonds also consider appearing in the telethon and give us their endorsement as well? Associating with the family's reputation for integrity and wholesomeness would be a big plus for any charity.

Like their sister, Alan and Merrill could not have been more receptive, or more agreeable with their reply. Yes, they told us, we could use the family studio again, rent free as before. And yes, this time the Osmond family would also agree to participate and lend its name to the cause. As with Marie, we couldn't even begin at that moment to appreciate what that collaboration would mean for the future.

(YOU GOTTA BE KIDDING!)

OSMOND ENTERTAINMENT   March 5, 1982

Mr. Joseph Lake
Associate Producer
MARCH OF DIMES
3539 South Main St.
Salt Lake City, UT   84115

Dear Joe:

     We have enjoyed the relationship and close association with
the March of Dimes for the past two years when it has been our privilege
to host the Miracle Network live from the Osmond Entertainment Center
here in Orem, Utah.

     During these broadcasts we have felt more and more confident in
the facilities and its capabilities to handle your demands and many
more. Needless to say, we are extremely proud of the Center, its technical prowess and the people who staff and control it.

     We simply want you to know that we stand ready to support you and
your team any way we can again in 1983 when, hopefully, the Miracle
Network will expand into even more market areas--bringing the high quality
of your production into millions of more homes. We were estatic about
the quality of your production this year AND the calibre of stars you
flew in for the broadcast. We have every reason to believe it will be
even bigger and better next year! You can't miss!

     Should there be any area at all we can assist in making this a
reality for your staff and the very premis of what the March of Dimes
stands for, don't hesitate to call upon us.

     Continued warm wishes to you and all who make "the miracle happen"
for these wonderful little children! Your work must be very satisfying
indeed!

                              Sincerely yours,

                              Alan R. Osmond

                              Merrill D. Osmond

ADO, MDO:kp

John Schneider with March of Dimes Patient

....

CHAPTER EIGHT

Was it Really That Good?

With the Osmond Studios and John and Marie secured, now we needed to see if anyone out there was willing to buy what we were selling.

I approached the people in Boise first. After the success of their participation in the 1981 telethon, I was confident both the March of Dimes chapter and television station KIVI would be eager to continue. Fortunately, they proved me right. But after that we had our work cut out for us. Recruiting local March of Dimes chapters wasn't a problem. Adding a telethon to their schedule meant finding more volunteers and increasing duties for the staff, but the fundraising potential made the expansion more than worth it. The potential reward was well worth the risk.

Recruiting TV stations, though, was a different story. Taking on the telethon meant giving up twenty-one hours of revenue-producing airtime over a Saturday night and Sunday, plus there was the added complication that many stations were already affiliated with a charity-oriented telethon and didn't want to host another. We lost out on the Denver market, for example, for that reason. The station we approached, an independent, already had a working agreement with the Easter Seals telethon, so even though the Colorado March of Dimes chapter was a go, the TV station was not.

We stayed away from big markets like Los Angeles, San Francisco, and Seattle because we knew those would be tougher sells for a regional telethon. Instead, Joe and I focused on several medium-sized markets in the western part of the country we thought we had a reasonable shot at getting. The plan called for each hour of the telecast to be divided into forty-five minutes for the regional show and fifteen minutes for local content. Of the money raised, sixty percent would go to the national March of Dimes and forty percent would as usual stay with the local chapter.

Of the markets we went after, we wound up getting ten. In addition to Salt Lake City, they included Boise, Las Vegas, Albuquerque, Fresno, Phoenix, Sacramento, Tucson, Tulsa, and San Diego. Tulsa was the only market outside the West and that happened because the Tulsa March of Dimes chapter recruited *us*. They heard what we were doing and on their own signed up a television station.

In terms of market size, Phoenix and San Diego were our biggest gets. Both of the stations also carried Jerry Lewis's Labor Day telethon benefiting Muscular Dystrophy, but didn't balk at adding us—an encouraging sign that telethon loyalty didn't have to be exclusive. It helped that both stations were ABC affiliates that had carried *Donny & Marie* when it was on the air and were familiar with the capabilities of the Osmond Studios.

We scheduled an intensive two-day training session for March of Dimes staff and the TV station producers at the Osmond Studios. This turned out to be a great opportunity for collaboration and suggestions. Al Henderson and Mike Mischler conducted the production sessions and quickly gained the respect of the TV station people. Over that two-day period, Marie and the Osmonds stepped in from time to time to add their support. As a result, we all wound up bonding into a team.

Capitalizing on our lineup of celebrity hosts and our venue at the Osmond Studios, Joe got busy assembling an entertainment lineup a cut above any previous broadcasts. Rather than concentrating only on talent that was connected in some way or another to the Utah region, he expanded his networking to Hollywood. Among those who agreed to be part of our expanded regional broadcast was a young Heather Locklear, who had just started out that fall in a TV show that would become a huge hit called *Dynasty*; Gordon Jump of *WKRP in Cincinnati* TV fame (Jump had participated earlier in our Utah-only telethons); pop singer Danny Deardorff, who had been confined to a wheelchair almost all his life because of polio; and Bill Christopher, who played Father Mulcahy on the television show M*A*S*H.

Actor Gary Collins agreed to M.C. the show. His wife, former Miss America Mary Ann Mobley, also committed to help host. Singer and Broadway star Maureen McGovern signed on, as did country singers Louise Mandrell and Dottie West. All the Osmonds, including Donny, agreed to perform.

To get our Los Angeles-based entertainers and celebrities—a group that included almost everyone except the Osmonds—to Utah, our plan was to charter a plane that would fly them to Salt Lake City, put them up in first-class accommodations at the Hilton Hotel in Salt Lake City, and provide them with limo service to and from the airport in Lincoln Town Cars.

The L.A.-to-Utah airfare was a big expense we weren't sure how we were going to pay for—until Pacific Southwest Airlines came forward almost at the last minute.

We had been introduced to the people at PSA through the San Diego March of Dimes chapter. On a whim, when the BYU football team traveled to San Diego to play in the 1981 Holiday Bowl on the Friday before Christmas, I set up a meeting with the airline at its office near Lindbergh Field. On the way I stopped by the Mission Bay Hilton, where the BYU team was staying, and picked up Jim McMahon to accompany me.

McMahon, you'll recall, had helped us with our Walkathon a year and a half earlier when he joined John Schneider on the KSL helicopter that traversed the state. Since that time McMahon had transformed into a bona fide college superstar. A year previous, in the 1980 Holiday Bowl, he had brought BYU back from certain defeat with a last-second fifty-five-yard Hail Mary touchdown pass to cap a furious rally that included three touchdowns in the last three minutes and fifty-six seconds. The 46-45 BYU victory took its place in the history books as one of the greatest comebacks in college football history. In the 1981 regular season, McMahon had guided the Cougars to a 10-2 record, yet another berth in the Holiday Bowl as conference champions, and set thirty-two NCAA records while throwing more touchdowns in a single season than any college quarterback ever.

Even though a big bowl game was coming up, when I asked Jim if he'd accompany me to my meeting at PSA, he said sure. He was in shorts and a T-shirt lounging by the pool when I came by the Hilton to pick him up.

McMahon was a man who conformed to no mold, and that turned out to be a perfect fit for an airline that conformed to no mold. PSA was nothing if not unconventional. Its motto was "The World's Friendliest Airline." They painted smiley faces on the front of all their planes. They took to the laidback McMahon like he was part of the family. By the time we were finished talking, they had offered us their luxury suite at Jack Murphy Stadium to watch the upcoming Holiday Bowl game. More importantly, they committed full use of one of their Boeing 737 airplanes to shuttle our entertainers back and forth from Burbank to Salt Lake City for the upcoming telethon, free of charge.

Two nights later, as my family and I enjoyed the lavish buffet spread that came with the PSA Suite at Jack Murphy Stadium while we watched McMahon and BYU, in another to-the-wire thriller, defeat Washington State by two points—I mused on the fact that PSA didn't even fly to Salt Lake City.

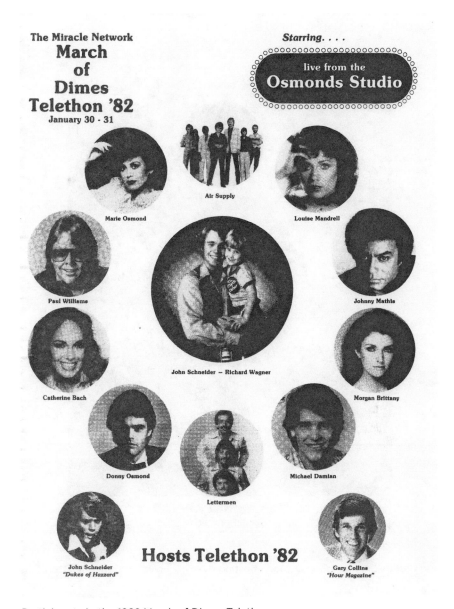

Participants in the 1982 March of Dimes Telethon

John Schneider and Marie Osmond hosting the 1982 March of Dimes Telethon

....

CHAPTER NINE

Rejected

No sooner had the 1982 telethon ended than I hoped it was as good as I thought it was.

Al Henderson, Mike Mischler, and the entire Video West crew ... John and Marie ... Gary Collins, Maureen McGovern, and all of the many entertainers and presenters ... the volunteers working the phone banks ... the ultra-professional Osmond Studios ... the expertly produced films highlighting that the cause was to fight birth defects and help kids—all, in my estimation, had nailed it.

The telecast started with a fair bit of drama. We were five minutes from going on air when Marie came on stage ready to open the show. Olive Osmond, Marie's mom, was sitting in the audience. She took one look at Marie's dress, with a long slit up one leg, and summoned her daughter off the stage. On the spot, Mrs. Osmond got out a needle and thread and then and there, calm as you please, sewed up the slit. Marie was not going on stage until her dress was deemed suitably modest by her mother.

With seconds to spare, Marie, as calm as her mother had been stitching that dress, walked on stage on time and on cue, and proceeded to belt out her opening number without a hitch.

From there, the telethon went on uninterrupted. For a maiden voyage there was little to complain about. There was a fair amount of improvising, especially when compared to later telethons. At one point, Alan, Wayne, Merrill, and Jay Osmond—the original Osmond Brothers—stayed on stage singing a medley for thirteen and a half minutes straight—an eternity in TV time. At another point, in the wee hours of the morning, I fell asleep backstage. Mike Mischler sneaked up and wrote in capital letters CALL NOW on the soles of my shoes. The camera zoomed in on my feet, reminding whoever was up watching at three in the morning that the phone lines were open.

For me, the experience was pure fun and gratifying both at the same time. I had lobbied hard for this; my neck was on the line and I knew it. If it flopped I had wasted the chapter's money and a year of everyone's time.

But everyone did their part. The hosts were professional and compassionate; Al and Mike worked their producing magic; the broadcast ratio of forty-five minutes for regional and fifteen minutes for local seemed to please everyone, with no transition blips to speak of. Best of all, donations poured in throughout the twenty-one hours. We raised more funds by far than any previous March of Dimes telethon.

Behind the scenes, the first-class treatment of the entertainers went off as planned. The rooms at the Hilton were excellent, the volunteer drivers in their Lincoln Town Cars delivered everyone on time where they were supposed to be, and when it was all over Sunday afternoon the Pacific Southwest Airlines 737 with the smiley face whisked all the celebrities back to Burbank. Before the Town Cars left the Osmond Studios, I got a chance to thank everyone and let them know they were all welcome to return the next year.

Sunday afternoon, I flew the fifty miles back to Salt Lake City on Chopper Five, KSL's helicopter, clutching the box of tapes the producers have given me of the broadcast. Once home,

I sat down and started watching every minute. Sleep deprived or not—the cat nap at three in the morning had been it for more than a day—I couldn't rest until I confirmed my belief that we had something of quality to offer. By Monday morning, I'd finished looking at the tapes—and was more convinced than ever.

Others soon chimed in. Every March of Dimes chapter that had signed on to the telecast called to say they were pleased with the impact the show had on their community. All had raised significant funds; all indicated they wanted to do it again.

Among our local group, the feeling was unanimous: we should definitely go national. Look at the exponential success we had expanding to just ten markets. Think what good we could do if we were in hundreds of markets all across the country. There's no reason our telethon couldn't be as big as Jerry Lewis's—or bigger.

Shortly after the telethon ended, Joe and I boarded a plane for New York City. We had asked for, and secured, a meeting at March of Dimes headquarters. Our briefcases were packed with a detailed proposal to present to senior management. It included all the essential elements associated with the production costs of a telethon, but with what we regarded as our ace in the hole: all the astonishing gifts-in-kind that were included. Free use of the Osmond Studios as our production facility was going to save the March of Dimes $300,000. The use of Bonneville's satellite uplink, and the subsequent free use of twenty-one hours of air time on the satellite, would save another $55,000. Add to that the donated air travel from PSA and other freebies from KSL and the point was obvious: we could do a national telethon for less than anyone else had ever done it.

We were put up in Manhattan at the historic Warwick Hotel on 54th Street, where the Beatles and Elvis Presley once stayed. The March of Dimes took care of the expenses. Joe and I did not have to share a room. The next morning a car picked us up in front of the hotel and whisked us an hour away to the March of Dimes headquarters in White Plains.

We met in a conference room with Bob Russell, executive vice president of the March of Dimes, and Ed Franck, vice president of communications. These were people I respected and admired; people I had worked with, if peripherally, for the past nine years. I was very familiar with Ed Franck's talent as a producer. I'd been using his films for years; all of it was first rate. The recent work he'd done with golfer Arnold Palmer and the kids at the children's hospital in Orlando was among the most incredible footage I'd ever seen.

Joe and I entered the room thinking slam dunk. We were fully confident we had an offer they couldn't refuse. We knew the national office had received letters of support from each of the ten chapters that had participated in the regional telecast. Mike Gursey and John Schneider had also sent a letter praising the telethon and urging it go national. On top of that, Utah had a sterling reputation in the March of Dimes family. In the previous year we had raised over $1 million for the charity—in a state with a population of one million people. Our one-dollar per capita average was by far tops in the country, well over the national average of twenty-one cents.

All was looking great when Russell and Franck started out by effusively praising our regional telethon and agreeing the time had come for the March of Dimes to go national.

But the air went out of the balloon very quickly when we were told they didn't want us to produce it, nor did they want the telethon to remain in Utah.

We were informed that in advance of our meeting, plans had already been put in motion to secure the Sunset Gower studios in Hollywood for the first national production. Ed Franck would head the effort, assembling a first-rate production crew to produce the telethon.

Joe and I were stunned. Rent for Sunset Gower for two weeks alone would be $300,000. There would be no free satellite connection, no free satellite uplink, no Al and Mike as producers. Everything we had built up would be lost. Money that could go directly to the kids was going to be diverted elsewhere.

The bottom line sunk in: national loved the concept and results; they didn't love the location. They asked Joe and I if we would be willing to move to Los Angeles and work with Ed Franck. That wasn't likely to happen. Our telethon was going Hollywood. We weren't.

On the quiet hour drive back to New York City, Joe and I tried to process what had just happened. By the time we arrived at the airport and boarded our flight, we each had the same concern: what were we going to tell our team that had poured heart and soul into the telethon—the show's hosts, the Osmond Studios, KSL and Videowest, PSA, the folks at the Utah chapter of the March of Dimes? How were we going to explain that the telethon as we knew it had been rejected, and it might all be over?

First Children's Miracle Network logo

....

CHAPTER TEN

Up in the Night

It was cold, late, and dark when we landed in Salt Lake and I made my way to my car in the parking lot. I'd spent the five-hour flight from New York City determined to figure out a way we could possibly continue, all to no avail. My mind was too jumbled. Back at home, exhausted and frustrated, I got into bed, hoping sleep would help. But I just stared at the ceiling. My mind racing a hundred miles an hour, I got out of bed, went to the kitchen table, pulled out a yellow legal pad, and started scribbling.

Was I a mad scientist? Or Just mad? After a few hours, wadded up pieces of yellow paper were tossed all around the room. But out of that mess the basics of a viable business model and financial model began to emerge.

My thoughts kept turning to Primary Children's Hospital in Salt Lake City. At the Utah chapter of the March of Dimes, that's where our forty percent of the funds we collected each year were allocated. Every cent that stayed local from Walk America, the Mothers March, the telethon, and all our other fundraising efforts, went to Primary Children's to support the birth defects programs there.

I jotted this down on the legal pad:

100 percent local

I asked myself, *What if we ran a charity that gave every cent of the funds raised in any given area to the local children's hospital?* There would be no sixty percent going to headquarters in New York City, as in the March of Dimes model. There would be no diversion of fundraising money at all. One hundred percent of money donated in Utah would stay in Utah, all of it going to Primary Children's. One hundred percent of money donated in Boise would stay in Boise, all of it going to St. Luke's. And so forth. All funds collected locally would stay local. Period.

Next I jotted down this word:

Network.

Now I mused, *What if we built a network that was made up exclusively of hospitals for children?* In most places the children's hospital is the most powerful nonprofit brand in the community. I knew this from personal experience. Children's hospitals take care of all children regardless of ability to pay, regardless of affliction. This would not be a disease-of-the-month-club type charity. All of the March of Dimes babies, all of the Jerry Lewis muscular dystrophy kids, all of the Easter Seals children with disabilities, all of the kids served by other telethons—each and every one is cared for at their local children's hospital. A network of children's hospitals would be a very powerful and appealing cause. It would encompass *all* health care for children. Everything would be for the kids.

Now I wrote:

Funding.

What if, I thought, *in order to pay the operating costs for a national office that would manage this new children's hospital network, we charged each member hospital a fee based on the size of its television market?* Toying with the numbers, next to New York City, the country's largest market, I wrote, "$25,000." Next to Boise, on the small end, I wrote "$9,000."

All other markets would fall somewhere in between according to their size.

Under this structure, each children's hospital in the network would "buy" the television market it belonged to—with the understanding, of course, that this upfront market fee would be more than made up for by funds allocated to the hospital at the conclusion of each year's telethon.

I searched for and found the Arbitron TV ratings system map that Al Henderson had given me. Every television market across the country was well defined—201 of them laid out coast to coast, from No. 1 New York City to No. 201 Roswell, New Mexico. Each one represented a potential spoke in the children's hospital network cog. I could foresee that some hospitals might be in a position where they would want to buy more than one TV market, but to maintain exclusivity, it made sense that no market ought to be owned by more than one hospital.

On the pages of the legal pad I sketched out three ways of raising money for the children's hospitals.

The first was the traditional telethon model of receiving telephone pledges from viewers who call the number on their TV screen during the twenty-one hours of programming.

The second was direct gifts from corporate sponsors. Contributions from local corporate sponsors would stay with the local hospital, while donations from national corporate sponsors would be distributed to all hospitals in the network on a percentage basis, the amounts determined according to market size. For example, if a national company such as Marriott gave, say, $300,000 to the network, each hospital would get a portion of the $300,000, with those in the larger markets such as New York getting a bigger share than those in the smaller markets such as Boise. The funds would be allocated based on the percentage of total U.S. TV households in each hospital's market.

The third means of fundraising I listed were special event fundraisers—walkathons, dance marathons, golf tournaments, bake sales, and so forth. These could be coordinated and conducted by the hospital staff in each local market, with how-to direction from the national office.

At the end of the night I looked at the scribbles on the legal pad. Less than twenty-four hours since Joe and I had sat at March of Dimes headquarters learning our telethon was going to be moved and produced by someone else, a new way of doing things had emerged. Would it work? **Never doubted it!** I felt what was on those pages was the very best formula possible. After nine years in the nonprofit sector, I was convinced that recruiting TV stations to carry the telethon for the local children's hospital was a more power and attractive proposition than any before it, especially with the promise that 100 percent of all funds raised locally would stay local. The key would be getting the TV stations to donate their air time. That was a big ask. But we had been able to do just that with the ten stations we'd recruited for the March of Dimes regional telethon.

It was no sure thing. Far from it. The truth was, what I'd sketched out had never been done in the history of philanthropy. The business and financial model was totally unique. TV stations, radio stations, sponsors, and organizations would be supporting their local hospital, not a national office. Managing this would require a tremendous amount of trust; it would need to be operated with the utmost integrity. All of our constituents would need to be convinced that this new network was the most effective, efficient opportunity for them to save lives and improve the quality of life for children.

The following best summarizes the conclusions I came to:

100 Percent of proceeds would stay local to benefit local hospitals and kids.

Kids first and always.

Maintain the lowest cost ratio possible.

Dignity and class always—
never exploit sick or injured kids.

In our former life, we had been the March of Dimes Make a Miracle Happen Telethon. In our new iteration we would be a network—a network of children's hospitals, and a network of television stations.

On the bottom of the legal pad the final thing I wrote was our new name:

Children's Miracle Network

(You gotta be kidding!)

Mick and Marilyn McCoo

....

CHAPTER ELEVEN

Plan B—The New Vision

I called Joe and immediately gathered up my yellow pads and took them straight to his house. I knew I couldn't do this without Joe. His connections and networking skills would be more invaluable and indispensable now than ever. And once again, I needed someone to tell me if I was crazy or not. Clearly, I was.

But I was pretty sure he'd be in. Joe lived for a good challenge. He loved taking a risk. And this was definitely a risk.

After I laid out my plans to him, true to form, he did not hesitate.

"If you think this will work," he said. "So do I."

Looking back, Joe's commitment was the single most important event in the history of Children's Miracle Network. And that's not even a close call. If not for his buy-in and expertise, nothing would have unfolded after that.

NO JOE! NO CMN!

We set up a makeshift office on two card tables in the basement of Joe's house, down the hall from his kids' bedrooms and across from the furnace room— the first headquarters of the Children's Miracle Network. We had no phone, no desks, no chairs, no bank account, no paychecks, and, some would say, no chance.

Going back home that first night, after spending the day working out some early logistical details with Joe, I started feeling guilty. I was making $35,000 a year working for the March of Dimes, nothing outrageous but a comfortable enough salary in 1982. Was I being selfish, giving up that security at my family's expense? Did I have a right to do that? Was I overreacting to a snub? Being too proud? We had some family savings, and had always stayed out of debt. But we could only survive for a few months before we'd be in the hole, and nobody had a clue when and where there might ever be a regular paycheck again.

Second-guessing myself, I went home and talked to my family. I laid out everything for my wife and kids—what I was proposing to do and why. I told them this couldn't be my decision only; we needed to be all in as a family. My kids were little. I'm sure none of them understood much of what I was talking about. But I'm confident they understood my passion and my conviction that this new idea of mine would be an even better way to help sick and injured children. Being on the front lines helping kids had shaped them just as it had shaped me. The vote to go with Dad's idea was unanimous.

Because of my great relationship and respect for our friends in Boise, I went to them quickly to share the concept and seek their advice. I saw Dr. Tom Wells and Dr. Dale Henken and Henrietta Andress at St. Luke's. All were enthusiastic supporters and the first to sign up to be part of the new network.

I next called KSL and set up an appointment with Arch Madsen, CEO of Bonneville Broadcasting, and Jay Lloyd, general manager of Bonneville's KSL-TV. They knew we'd been to New York.

"So, how'd it go?" they asked.

"Well…they don't want us," I said.

They were just as incredulous—to my great relief—as I was. These were television pros who knew firsthand what KSL and Bonneville had been giving every year to the March of Dimes telethon. The uplink and use of the satellite, the air time, the producers and production crew, those were huge contributions that saved tens of thousands of dollars. But to KSL it had always been worth it because the cause was worth it. They had loyally supported the March of Dimes telethon for going on twenty years, long before I came to town. But now...No one said it in so many words, they were far too professional for that, but it was hard not to take New York's decision as an insult, a slap in the face.

If we wanted to go a different route, they said they would go with us. KSL was on board to air the first Children's Miracle Network telethon—if there actually was one.

Joe and I understood that our new telethon, to have a fighting chance, needed to look like our old telethon. We couldn't change the formula and we couldn't change the format. That meant recruiting our talent pool all over again. We needed to convert them all.

The first person we needed to talk to was John Schneider.

At the meeting in New York, the March of Dimes had made it clear they wanted John to host their national telethon and also continue to serve as their Walk America chairman. He was one part of the show that they wanted to keep.

But we needed him too, more than ever, and he couldn't very well do both.

Upon hearing of our NEW VISION, Mike Gursey, John's manager, flew to Salt Lake City to hear it for himself. Mike had learned through the grapevine that the word from March of Dimes leadership was that John and Mike "Will do what we want them to do." When Mike related that information to John, John said, "F---- 'em, we're going with Mick and Joe."

Leaving nothing to chance, and knowing we had to talk to John in person, Joe and I found ourselves back on the I-15 freeway to Los Angeles. Just like a year ago, we rented a car and shared a room at the same cheap Howard Johnson's off the 101 in Hollywood, only now the charges went on our own credit cards. Fortunately, being debt adverse all my life, mine had its full $10,000 limit. But who knew how long that would last?

We met John at his apartment in Toluca Lake across the mountain from Hollywood. He and Mike Gursey sat on the couch across from Joe and me. The irony of the situation did not escape any of us. We had introduced John to the March of Dimes; in no time at all he had become the face of the charity; his picture was on billboards and 7-Eleven cups all over America; he had helped raise millions of dollars in the fight against birth defects—and now we were here to lure him away.

"They still want you," we told him. "But they don't want us."

We laid out our plan to go in a different direction; to set up a nationwide network of children's hospitals. We wanted John to be the face of *that*. With his help and endorsement, we told him, we believed we had the potential to do something really significant. Mike Gursey, who had already been briefed about all this earlier in Salt Lake City, sat back and didn't say anything. This was John's decision.

When we'd finished sharing our new vision, John looked at Mike and then turned to us. He said that the reason he was with the March of Dimes was because of the personal relationship he had with us.

"We're a team," he said.

Joe and I let out a huge sigh of relief. I firmly believe had John Schneider not stayed with us we may have given up before we ever got started. He was that important to our moving forward. **NO JOHN! NO CMN!**

Next, just as importantly, we needed his co-host and counterpart, Marie Osmond.

Marie was sitting with her manager Karl Engemann in the green room of the Osmond Studios when Joe and I, after rushing home from California, met with her in Orem. We delivered the same passionate message we'd just given to John. Without hesitation, she delivered the same response. Absolutely, she wanted to continue with the team. Her participation in the recent telethon was fresh on her mind. Marie had positively beamed as she held the miracle babies. Being involved in a cause that benefited children's hospitals was something she could dedicate herself to heart, soul, and mind. Of course she also had no problem choosing the Osmond Studios over Hollywood. **NO MARIE! NO CMN!**

Like John, Marie asked for nothing for herself. Neither of them ever would. The buy-in from the two of them gave us the credibility, and the energy, to move forward. It's impossible to understate that. These two young entertainers possessed impeccable character and reputation, and would never embarrass us. **They were founders of the Children's Miracle Network every bit as much as Joe Lake and me.**

After getting Marie's commitment, we went to Merrill's office and met with Merrill and his brother Alan about again using the Osmond Studios.

The brothers couldn't have been more supportive. Our relationship with the March of Dimes may have changed, but they assured us our relationship with the Osmonds had not. They promised us continued full run of their studio for our telethon, just as before, and the full support of the family.

As we were discussing the possibilities for the future, they mentioned the existence of the Osmond Foundation.

The two oldest Osmond brothers, Tom and Virl, suffered from speech and hearing impairments. Olive Osmond, in an effort to teach the family to give back, set up a foundation to support those impacted by speech and hearing problems. They called it the Osmond Foundation for the Children of the World and suggested it was available if it would be helpful to affiliate our charity with the foundation. We gave some thought to the possibility, but by 1982 the Osmond's foundation was no longer active and had not maintained its 501(c)(3) nonprofit IRS status. The foundation's staff had not filed their 990 tax returns for two years. It turned out not to be a practical alternative, and Children's Miracle Network became the primary brand of the organization. But as we would realize many times over in the years to come, the gesture was typical of the Osmonds: whatever was theirs was yours too. In building the Children's Miracle Network, the Osmond name, reputation, and image, was a powerful asset. (**YOU GOTTA BE KIDDING!**)

It was painful for me to resign from the March of Dimes. I considered it to be the best-run, most efficient nonprofit out there. I had enormous respect for the entire organization. For nine very good, very productive years they had been nothing but good to my family and me. However, it was clearly time to go.

The reaction from March of Dimes headquarters was the same as my reaction to them not wanting to do our telethon: *Are you nuts?! You want to start a new charity?* I couldn't blame them. These were people who knew how challenging it was to run a successful national charitable organization. (The national March of Dimes wound up holding their telethon in Los Angeles, but they only did the one show and it didn't work out for them; I'm not sure all the reasons why).

I got more sympathy from the Utah March of Dimes chapter. I had grown close to the Board, in particular Sherry Shelton and Fred Ferre, who were gracious and understanding about my leaving. Sherry and Fred made up a little plaque they presented to me as a parting gift. It read: *Dazzle them with brilliance; or baffle them with bullshit!* It was the first thing I hung on the wall once I had an office to hang it in.

That office ended up being in some donated space above the Brighton Bank building in the middle of the Salt Lake Valley. Jim Fraser, the bank president, was a neighbor and friend of mine and one of the first people Joe and I invited to be on the inaugural CMN Board of Trustees. Assembling a Board was among our very first priorities. If I knew anything, I knew how critical Board oversight is to an organization, especially a nonprofit. Our choice for chairman was J. Gary Sheets, a local businessman. Gary, who grew up in rural Utah, had pulled himself up by the bootstraps to establish a very successful financial services company with clients throughout the Intermountain West. He knew what it was to start something from scratch. When he listened to our idea of inventing a new national charity, he said yes immediately. Others on that first Board were Alan Tibbitts, David Monson, Kent Norton, Fred L. Smith, Mark Van Wagoner, Stephen O. Behunin, Chris Corey, Marie Osmond, and Bonnie Karigan, who served as secretary. They were a cross-section of local business and political leaders. Notes from the first Board meeting show that we had a starting balance of $488.34. I have no recollection of where that came from!

So we were organized. We had a Board of Trustees. We had a telethon and a place to host the broadcast. We even had a bank account. But all the plans and organizing and talent wouldn't mean anything if the Children's Miracle Network didn't have an actual network. That meant Joe and I needed to reach out to the children's hospitals across America and Canada. Could we convince them we were worth their time? Could we talk them into joining something that was untried and untested? That's what we were about to find out.

John Schneider, Marilyn McCoo and Merlin Olsen

....

CHAPTER TWELVE

Merlin & Marilyn

In strategizing to expand the telethon, Joe and I conjured up an A list of celebrities we felt would work well alongside John and Marie as co-hosts. The idea was to add diversity and variety, with an aim at appealing to an ever-widening audience.

We drove back to Los Angeles to see if we could get the first two names on our list.

Our first stop was the Sunset Gower Studios in Hollywood—the very studios where the March of Dimes planned to host its first national telethon. The studios, located on the corner of Sunset Boulevard and Gower Street, had a rich history. Major motion pictures like *The Caine Mutiny*, *Funny Girl*, and *Mr. Smith Goes to Hollywood* had been produced at the fourteen-acre lot back when it was owned by Paramount. Now it produced independent television productions, including *Solid Gold*, a popular weekly top-of-the-charts music show. *Solid Gold* was hosted by Andy Gibb of the Bee Gees and Marilyn McCoo—the person we had come to see.

Marilyn McCoo had won her fame as lead singer of the 5th Dimension, a group that produced a string of hits in the 1960s and 1970s like *One Less Bell to Answer*, *Wedding Bell Blues*, *and Stoned Soul Picnic*. The group's signature hit was *Up, Up and Away*, a song that would go on to assume a special place in Children's Miracle Network lore. But that's getting ahead of the story. In the spring of 1982, when Joe and I were ushered into her dressing room at Sunset Gower Studios, we knew much more about Marilyn McCoo than she knew about us.

Joe had met Marilyn and her husband, Billy Davis Jr., the man who started the 5th Dimension, when Sunshade 'n Rain, the Utah band Joe managed, had opened in Las Vegas for the 5th Dimension. Everything about the couple had impressed him. They were a singing duo now, having moved on from their 5th Dimension days. They were devout Christians with a reputation for helping good causes and giving back. And as African-American entertainers they would bring a diversity that would be important for a national telethon. Our hope was that Marilyn would agree to a co-hosting role alongside Marie, and Billy would agree to participate in the telethon as an entertainer.

I'd always heard about star power. That day I saw it when thirty-seven-year-old Marilyn McCoo walked into her studio dressing room—a star in every sense of the word, the kindest, sweetest, most intelligent, articulate, humble, in-control woman you could ever hope to meet.

What I remember most about that day is how, after we'd been introduced, and even though she'd already been briefed by her people about our cause, Marilyn interviewed *us*. She must have asked questions for thirty minutes straight. When she was satisfied she flashed her million-dollar smile and said, yes, she and Billy would participate in the telethon, and she would be happy to help out as a co-host.

The next morning, we drove to Simi Valley.

Simi Valley was where Big Sky Ranch was located, the film studio where the TV show *Little House on the Prairie* was shot. Merlin Olsen, one of *Little House's* stars and the next name on our list, had agreed to meet us between takes. A day earlier, I'd never been on a movie set in my life; now I was visiting my second, and about to shake the biggest hand I'd ever encountered in my life.

I reached out for a handshake and watched my own hand disappear.

Huge. No word ever described a person better than that one word described Merlin Olsen. He was huge in every sense of his life. At six-foot-two and two hundred and seventy pounds, he'd won the Outland Trophy, the award given to the top lineman in college football, when he played for Utah State, his hometown team. In the National Football League, as part of the fabled Fearsome Foursome of the Los Angeles Rams, he was named All-Pro fourteen consecutive seasons—still a record. He was inducted into the NFL Hall of Fame the first year he was eligible. The state of Utah named him its Athlete of the Century.

Hardly content to rest on his football laurels, Merlin didn't miss a step when his playing career was over. He became an award-winning television commentator, working alongside Dick Enberg and other play-by-play announcers at Super Bowls and hundreds of professional and college football games with his deep baritone voice. And when Hollywood came calling to see if he could act, well, he could do that too.

In *Little House*, Merlin played the role of Jonathan Garvey, sidekick to Charles Ingalls, the lead role played by Michael Landon. There was a break in the shooting when Joe and I arrived, which is when Merlin walked up to us and shook our hands.

But big as he was, there was nothing overpowering about Merlin Olsen. He didn't intimidate people; he didn't belittle or make you feel small. When you were in his presence you felt immediately relaxed. Comfortable. Secure. Merlin Olsen was as genuine as he was accomplished. FTD Florists, the national flower delivery company, used him as their spokesperson. Here was a giant of the gridiron people believed in so completely he could sell flowers!

He wasn't a singer or a dancer, he didn't have a hit record, but it was simple why we wanted Merlin to be a co-host of the telethon: how could anyone not think it was legit if he was part of it?

It was always straightforward with Merlin, always easy, never complicated. In all the years he worked with us, he never asked for anything, no handlers, no special privileges, no extra attention; he'd just show up with a single bag slung over his shoulder.

I remember sitting down with him that day and simply saying, "It's for the kids."

For Merlin, that was enough. When Joe suggested he might want to take some time and think it over before he gave us his answer, he shrugged his shoulders and said, "I don't need to think about it."

Merlin being Merlin, he didn't rush us out of there. He took Joe and me onto the set and talked about the production as he showed us around, acting like he had all the time in the world. I remember seeing Michael Landon off to the side. When we said our goodbyes, Merlin stuck out that enormous hand of his and said, "Let me know when you need me."

It had been a remarkably productive trip. We were just two guys from Utah, pitching an untried idea to people who were megastars, and they were sending us back with total support for what we were doing, asking for nothing in return. (**YOU GOTTA BE KIDDING!**)

We got back on the I-15 freeway and headed north. Joe said to step on it. He'd phoned ahead and arranged backstage passes for us for the Wayne Newton show at the Aladdin. Yes, Joe Lake knew Wayne Newton's handlers. Approaching the Nevada state border, at about one hundred miles an hour, suddenly, unexpectedly, in the rearview mirror, right on top of us: lights and sirens. The cop had creeped up from behind without his lights on. That ended up being a $280 spending ticket. Way back then. For the longest time I was really careful driving in California after that. Maybe I should think about paying that ticket.

Rand O'Donnell, CEO of Arkansas Children's Hospital, one of the first hospitals to participate in 1982

....

CHAPTER THIRTEEN

Courageous and Caring

Joe and I parked just outside the iconic Paramount Pictures gate in Hollywood and stopped at the guard station. Did we have an appointment? Yes, we did. We had a meeting scheduled with Chuck Velona, general manager of KHJ-Channel 9, the television station that had offices on the Paramount lot.

How Joe got the meeting I did not know and I did not ask, but I was becoming more convinced by the day that the man could schmooze and talk his way into anything. The guard waved us through. Both of us were uncharacteristically nervous. We had Boise in the network, but nobody would care. Los Angeles was critical. We knew how valuable it would be, in terms of prestige as well as size, if the Children's Miracle Network could get the L.A. market—"The Entertainment Capital of the World." If you can make it in L.A. you can make it anywhere.

An amiable man with a ready smile, Chuck welcomed us into his office and listened attentively to our sales pitch. He visibly perked up when we explained that 100 percent of the proceeds raised locally would stay local. That was proving to be a very effective selling point. We weren't asking for anything for Children's Miracle Network. Every cent raised in Los Angeles, thanks to KHJ's broadcast, would go directly to the local children's hospital, which Chuck assumed was L.A.

Children's, the largest children's hospital in Los Angeles. And even though we hadn't in fact talked to L.A. Children's yet, we did not dispose him of that assumption. We were putting the cart before the horse, making it up as we went. But it wasn't the first time we'd winged it. As soon as Joe got the meeting with a station the caliber of KHJ we jumped at it.

The more he talked, the more I could see Chuck's bald scalp begin to perspire. He rubbed his hand over his head. I didn't take that as a good sign. But then he explained his consternation. Something inside him clicked when we talked about helping sick kids.

"I've got to do this," he said. "But guys...come on...give me a break! I am under contract to air religious programming on Sunday mornings. If I preempt those shows for your telethon, I will have to write a check back to those producers for $50,000. Is there any way you can get me $50,000 so we can go ahead and do this?"

Joe and I looked at each other, not quite believing what we'd just heard. True, best case scenario was getting the twenty-one hours of programming donated by the station. We couldn't afford to pay for air time in every market. But this was Los Angeles. We *needed* Los Angeles. Now we'd just learned we could have it. For a price.

"We'll get you the $50,000," I said as we shook on the deal, not giving Chuck the chance to change this mind. We had no idea how we were going to get the money. Then again, we had no idea how we were going to pay for a lot of things. But twenty-one hours of live TV in Los Angeles for $50,000? (**YOU GOTTA BE KIDDING!**) We are going to do that all day long.

Next we went to Children's Hospital Los Angeles on Sunset Boulevard, where their CEO agreed to meet with us. This was a tougher sell. Big hospitals like L.A. Children's were already raising tens of millions of dollars before we came along. What we were offering in the way of additional revenue from a new unproven telethon wasn't a huge selling point, particularly when we mentioned that, in addition to some other expenses, KHJ would need $50,000. Further complicating things, L.A. Children's had a reputation of avoiding connections to Hollywood entertainers, and this was definitely a Hollywood type deal we were presenting. We didn't walk out with a yes, but we didn't walk out with a no, either. They said they'd have to think about it.

We made sure they knew they were tops on our list. But we also left them with the thought that if they weren't interested, we would talk to their competitor, the Children's Hospital at UCLA, making sure they realized that whatever hospital signed with Children's Miracle Network would exclusively own the local broadcasting market. There was no threat implied, just letting them know that there were two great children's hospitals in Los Angeles to pick from.

After a few weeks L.A. Children's called to say they'd thought it over and they were in. A new CEO, Jane Hurd, had been hired in the interim who saw the value in a relationship that, beyond fundraising, could be positive for the hospital's marketing and branding. (Jane would later become a member of our Board. She was an amazing leader and contributor to the development of Children's Miracle Network). The L.A. negotiation taught us two valuable lessons we would remember in our future sales calls. One is that marketing, and the exposure that comes with it, can be just as important to a hospital, if not more important, as fundraising. And Two, the healthcare industry is very competitive.

Going national meant calling people we'd never met in places we'd never been. On one such cold call, a man named Larry Woodard answered the phone at Arkansas Children's Hospital in Little Rock. He was as unprepared for what I was about to ask for as I was for what he was about to give.

Larry was the development officer at Arkansas Children's. After hearing me out on the phone, he was interested enough to invite me to come to Little Rock for a meeting.

I flew into Little Rock by way of about five cities and checked into a hotel in the downtown area. That night my rental car got broken into. The thief had no idea he'd made such a poor choice. There was nothing worth stealing in the car.

Larry caught the vision immediately. He could see that the relationship we were offering had a tremendous upside in terms of exposure for the hospital. He said he would set up meetings for us with all three of Little Rock's network television stations. (In 1982 the three major networks, ABC, NBC, and CBS, were mostly all there was.) I came back a couple of weeks later. Arkansas Children's Hospital knew what they were doing. They brought along a member of the hospital Board who owned a number of large car dealerships and was the biggest advertiser in the market. With him in the room, all three stations said yes. (**YOU GOTTA BE KIDDING!**) Arkansas Children's could only sign with one, but they had their pick.

Larry was not through helping. He suggested we might want to go to Chicago to a children's hospital convention hosted by the National Association of Children's Hospitals and Related Institutions—NACHRI for short. It would give us an opportunity to talk to a lot of hospitals all at the same time.

Larry and Rand O'Donnell, the Arkansas Children's Hospital CEO, reserved a room at the convention site and invited some of their counterparts from around the country to sit in.

Joe and I flew into Chicago with reinforcements: John Schneider agreed to come with us. About thirty development officers and hospital CEOs filed into the meeting room for our presentation. The expressions on their faces were skeptical. What on earth could we offer them that they hadn't been offered before? And what was the TV star doing up there?

After a brief introduction, I began to explain the purpose for this meeting and introduced everyone there to the concept of the Children's Miracle Network. They were immediately impressed that we were committed to the pledge that 100 percent of proceeds would stay in *their* market to benefit *their* hospitals and *their* kids. We explained the fee schedule and asked for feedback and their reaction to that approach—suggesting the smallest market might pay $9,000 a year and the biggest might pay $25,000 a year. Several of the hospitals represented indicated they were ready to join Children's Miracle Network immediately. And in the next few years every one of the hospitals in that room joined the network.

Convincing hospitals to commit time and resources to something new and untested was difficult enough. They would be pioneers. But the really tough sell would be TV stations. These weren't healthcare providers, these were business people, and a telethon was about generating good will and providing a community service more than it was about profits. Once station managers caught the vision of helping kids in the local community, as Chuck Velona had in L.A., they were sold, but it was often hard to get the conversation that far. The Osmonds' image and reputation and the Osmond Studios proved to be a valuable asset.

In Columbus, Ohio, the Children's Hospital of Columbus had reached out to us to be part of the network and telethon. Knowing they needed a TV station to be involved, they offered to pay Joe's airfare to come to Columbus and make a presentation to WBNS, the CBS affiliate there. The hospital made an appointment for Joe to accompany Alan Brass, the hospital foundation's president, to meet with Gene D'Angelo, WBNS's President and General Manager. Columbus Children's Hospital did not even consider approaching another station. It was the powerhouse WBNS or no one. Gene had great respect for Jay Lloyd and KSL in Salt Lake City.

WBNS and Columbus Children's Hospital had a very strong relationship, similar to Primary Children's Hospital and KSL in Salt Lake City. Given that relationship, and Joe's inspired presentation, Gene and WBNS were a go.

Again, the game-changer was 100 Percent Stays Local. Gene's attitude changed dramatically when he understood that everything raised in Columbus would stay in Columbus; each and every dollar pledged would go directly to the Children's Hospital of Columbus. (Later on, Gene would become a member of the CMN Board of Governors. And if you're a movie-goer and the name rings a bell, it's because Gene's daughter, Beverly D'Angelo, is an actress who starred with Chevy Chase in the *Vacation* movies).

Slowly but surely, one buy-in at a time, our hospital network lineup grew. It started, appropriately enough, with St. Luke's in Boise, my old stomping grounds. That was my first visit. Joe's first visit was to University of California-Davis Medical Center in Sacramento. They signed up too. Those were the first two hospitals in Children's Miracle Network. That first year we wound up getting children's hospitals in all ten of the markets that had been part of our regional broadcast in '82. In addition to that was Los Angeles, our crown jewel; Columbus, Ohio; and, thanks to the initial support of Arkansas Children's and the meeting with the host of development officers in Chicago, a surprising number of children's hospitals in the Southeast. All told, by the time we were finished crisscrossing the country, we had twenty-two hospitals in the network, and thirty television markets.

These were the pioneer hospitals:

- Primary Children's Hospital, *Salt Lake City, Utah*
- St. Luke's Hospital, *Boise, Idaho*
- Los Angeles Children's Hospital, *Los Angeles, California*
- UC Davis Children's Hospital, *Sacramento, California*
- Arkansas Children's Hospital, *Little Rock. Arkansas*
- Children's Hospital of Alabama, *Birmingham, Alabama*
- Phoenix Children's Hospital, *Phoenix, Arizona*
- University of Arizona Children's Hospital, *Tucson, Arizona*

- San Diego Children's Hospital, *San Diego, California*
- Valley Children's Hospital, *Fresno, California*
- University of New Mexico Children's Hospital, *Albuquerque, New Mexico*
- Providence Hospital, *El Paso, Texas*
- University of Nevada Medical Center, *Las Vegas, Nevada*
- Columbus Children's Hospital, *Columbus, Ohio*
- Dayton Children's Hospital, *Dayton, Ohio*
- Beaumont Children's Hospital, *Detroit, Michigan*
- Vanderbilt Children's Hospital, *Nashville, Tennessee*
- East Tennessee Children's Hospital, *Knoxville, Tennessee*
- Akron Children's Hospital, *Akron, Ohio*
- Children's Hospital of Wisconsin, *Milwaukee, Wisconsin*
- Gillette Children's Hospital, *Minneapolis, Minnesota*
- Kapiolani Children's Hospital, *Honolulu, Hawaii*

These were the television stations:
- KIVI in Boise, *Idaho*
- KHJ in Los Angeles, *California*
- WKBD in Detroit, *Michigan*
- WAKC in Akron, *Ohio*
- WXIA in Atlanta, *Georgia*
- WSTP in Minneapolis, *Minnesota*
- KXTV in Sacramento, *California*
- KTSP in Phoenix, *Arizona*
- KSMB in San Diego, *California*
- WISN in Milwaukee, *Wisconsin*
- WTVS in Nashville, *Tennessee*
- WBNS in Columbus, *Ohio*
- KSL in Salt Lake City, *Utah*
- WHIO in Dayton, *Ohio*
- WVTM in Birmingham, *Alabama*
- KOTV in Tulsa, *Oklahoma*
- KTHV in Little Rock, *Arkansas*
- KOB in Albuquerque, *New Mexico*

- WBIR in Knoxville, *Tennessee*
- KFSN in Fresno, *California*
- KVOA in Tucson, *Arizona*
- KHON in Honolulu, *Hawaii*
- KVBC in Las Vegas, *Nevada*
- KVIA in El Paso, *Texas*
- KPOM in Fort Smith, *Arkansas*
- WAAY in Huntsville, *Alabama*
- WALA in Mobile, *Alabama*
- WUPU in Toledo, *Ohio*
- KIDO in Idaho Falls, *Idaho*
- WHEC In Rochester, *New York*

It's only a dollar. Buy a balloon.

....

CHAPTER FOURTEEN

Corporate America Made it Happen

After the meetings in Los Angeles with KHJ and L.A. Children's, Joe had set up another meeting, this one with an executive named Linda Dozier, vice president of public relations and communications for Western Airlines. Western, which would be acquired by Delta Airlines later in the decade, had its headquarters at LAX. The airline had a major hub in Salt Lake City. If you were traveling in and out of Salt Lake in the 1980s, Western was the airline to fly. One of our Board members, Bonnie Karigan, was general manager at the Hilton Hotel in Salt Lake City and had helped us secure some free flights on Republic Airlines, a regional carrier that flew in and out of Salt Lake. But Republic's flights were irregular and usually involved flying a number of connections to get where we wanted to go. Sometimes it took almost as long to fly, or longer, as it would have to drive. Flying **Western** Airlines was the only practical option.

When Linda Dozier, a professional in every sense of the word, came in and sat down on the other side of the desk, my right leg was going up and down like a metronome. Joe, who was intimidated by nobody, ever, reached over and put his hand on my knee so I would stop thumping. We told Linda we had driven from Utah to see her and we sure could use her help to get our charity off the ground. To our amazement, before we stood up we had a deal: free airfare for Joe and me, anytime, anywhere. Western Airlines had just made Salt Lake City a hub and was very familiar with Primary Children's Hospital and with KSL-TV. We had Los Angeles and Salt Lake, Western's two biggest markets. It was a savvy business decision. But for us, it was invaluable. (**YOU GOTTA BE KIDDING!**)

From then on, until Western merged with Delta five years later, we flew free. Not only that, they let us keep our miles!

Our next objective would have to be to find help with lodging when we were on the road selling our new concepts. Bill Marriott was CEO of the Marriott Corporation, the multi-national hotel company started by his father, J. Willard Marriott. Joe Lake, as it happened, had grown up in Salt Lake three houses away from Donna Garff, Bill Marriott's wife. As always, Joe's connections got us the appointment.

Bill had tremendous respect for Marie and the Osmond family. Joe and Marie flew to Washington, D.C. to meet with Bill at Marriott's Bethesda headquarters. They shared their passion for this new charity that would always put kids first. They talked about the values and principles that would govern the effort. Joe explained we had no funding. Western had agreed to provide complimentary flights for Mick and Joe to travel and share this vision. Marie asked if Marriott would consider providing free hotel rooms as we traveled. Without hesitation, Bill said, "Absolutely. That's something I would really like to do." (**YOU GOTTA BE KIDDING!**)

The generosity of Bill Marriott and **Marriott Hotels** and Linda Dozier and **Western Airlines** cannot be overstated in explaining how CMN was able to survive in the very lean early years. It's hard to imagine making it without their support. **NO MARRIOTT! NO WESTERN! NO CMN!**

But we still had bills to pay. Our only source of revenue to keep the lights on and pay the ongoing expenses required to run the organization was the approximately $240,000 in fees we were collecting from our member hospitals. Those fees were coming in slowly. We were able to hire a very talented young man by the name of Mike Reese for next to nothing, who proved to be a real jack of all trades. He got a lot of things done for us, including invoicing and managing the fee collection process from the hospitals. Still, as the inaugural CMN telethon approached, it became increasingly obvious that by themselves the fees weren't going to be nearly enough to cover all our mounting expenses. The $300,000 we were saving in rent at the Osmond Studios was a lifesaver, but that didn't cover production costs such as paying the studio musicians, makeup artists, and wardrobe people.

What we needed was a corporate partner who could bridge the funding gap. For months we had been trying to find one, to no avail. The problem was, all we had to sell was a vision and a dream. Children's Miracle Network wasn't on anyone's map. Our track record was nonexistent. A vision and a dream is very difficult to sell.

Then one day out of the blue Joe got a call from Clancy Isaac. Clancy ran an advertising and public relations agency in Columbus, Ohio. Columbus Children's Hospital was an inaugural member of CMN and WBNS, the CBS affiliate in Columbus, was one of the thirty television markets signed up to broadcast the 1983 telethon. At Joe's request, Clancy had been on the lookout for a company to help us with sponsorship. Huffy Bicycles was one of Clancy's clients and he thought a children's charity might be a good fit for a company that made children's bikes. Joe flew to Ohio to meet with the Huffy people at their headquarters in Dayton. Unfortunately, they declined to get involved, and Joe, by now used to rejection, went back to Columbus to stay the night before flying back to Utah the next morning.

That evening, Clancy called Joe in his room. He'd thought of one more client he felt Joe should see before he left. Figuring it couldn't hurt, Joe changed his flight and extended his stay one more day.

Duff's Smorgasbord was a chain of buffet restaurants owned by Homer and Wilma Duff. Duff's started out as a true mom-and-pop enterprise. Homer was running a grocery store in 1967 when he decided to open a deli in a corner of the store. His food was such a hit that by 1983 that deli had grown into one hundred-forty Duff's franchises located throughout the Midwest. The president of Duff's was a young Columbus lawyer named Brett Hutchens who had been instrumental in managing the growth that had led to the company's success.

Joe and Clancy drove to Cincinnati to meet with Homer and Brett. Joe laid out all our hopes and dreams for CMN. He told them we would be broadcasting from the Osmond Studios and the Osmond family was fully behind what we were doing. He promised that any company that paid $150,000 to sponsor the production would have their name prominently displayed and mentioned throughout the twenty-one hour telethon. It was the same pitch we'd been making for a year. His expectations were low to non-existent.

But there were a few things Joe didn't know.

He didn't know that just a few months earlier, Homer had told Brett he wanted to find a charity the company could become associated with. Homer and Wilma were at a stage in their lives when they were in a position to give back and they wanted to identify a good cause they could get behind and support.

He didn't know that Homer and Wilma were big fans of the Osmonds. They enjoyed their music and admired their family values.

Nor did he know that one of Brett Hutchens's children had recently been born with a heart defect and had spent a week at Cincinnati Children's Hospital for extra care before going home. There were no complications and the child was fine now, but the experience was an eye-opener for Brett about the critical importance of children's healthcare. He prayed and vowed if there was anything he could do to help with newborn care in the future, he would do so.

After Joe's presentation, Homer and Brett excused themselves and went out in the hall to talk.

"Homer, what do you think?" asked Brett.

"Well," Homer answered, "If I were going to donate to a cause, children's hospitals is a good place to do it. And if the Osmond family is involved, it's got to be a good thing."

"I feel the same way," said Brett.

They decided they could come up with the $150,000 to underwrite the telethon by getting commitments of about $1,000 from each of Duff's one hundred forty franchisees. And if some of the franchisees chose not to participate, Homer and Brett agreed they would personally come up with the balance.

The fact that they only had stores in seven of our telethon markets did not play a part in their decision. They weren't participating to help grow their company; they were participating to help children.

Homer and Brett walked back in the room and practically floored Joe when they told him, "We have a deal."

"How much would you like to sponsor?" asked Joe.

"All of it," they answered. (**YOU GOTTA BE KIDDING!**)

Joe couldn't wait to call me with the good news. Finally, we had a sponsor. Its name, he told me, was Duff's Smorgasbord.

Joe's enthusiasm was quickly countered by my skepticism.

"Who?" was my first response," followed closed with, "Why on earth would they do that?"

Why would a restaurant chain in Ohio we'd never heard of give $150,000 to a charity that had little connection to where their stores were located?

On paper, it was too good to be true. In reality, it was as real as real gets.

In the years to come, corporate America would step up in a big way for Children's Miracle Network. Walmart. Costco. RE/MAX. Dairy Queen. Marriott. Disney. Ace Hardware. Delta

Airlines. The McLane Company. Speedway...and many more. The list is impressive and lengthy, each company contributing time, resources, innovation, and funding to form the lifeblood of the cause. But Duff's Smorgasbord was the first. Without its show of support, the others might never have had a chance to follow.

Bit by bit, in fits and starts, the CMN community grew that first year. To help with our courting of corporate sponsors, Joe felt we needed a big celebrity support behind us and went to work compiling a VIP letterhead. Back in the days when people wrote letters on paper, an impressive letterhead—with names of important people lining the side of the stationery—could be a valuable asset in impressing people and closing deals. One of the first people who gave Joe permission to use his name was Gerald Ford, the former president who Joe had known during his days in politics. Gerald Ford's name went on the letterhead alongside John Schneider, Merlin Olsen, Marilyn McCoo, and all the Osmonds.

But the celebrity Joe most wanted was Bob Hope, America's favorite comedian. Marie Osmond and Bob Hope had a great relationship that dated back to when Marie first started appearing on his Christmas television specials as a young girl.

Joe asked Marie for her help. She was scheduled to appear on the 1982 Bob Hope Christmas TV special in December. Could she possibly introduce Joe to Hope? Each guest on the show was allowed to have one person accompany them backstage. Usually, Marie went with Karl Engemann, her longtime manager. But Marie arranged for Joe to take Karl's place.

Before they went on the set, Marie gave Joe his instructions: "Don't say a thing to Bob; don't talk to him at all. I will talk to him and at some point you and I will go into his dressing room and then you can ask him what you want to ask."

The scenario played out just as Marie had said it would. Once they were in the dressing room, Joe got his chance. He explained what CMN was all about and asked if Bob Hope would consider adding his name to the new charity's letterhead.

It certainly wasn't the first time Bob Hope had been hit up by a charity. All his life, he had helped others. His visits to entertain the troops—a tradition that started during World War II and never ended—were legendary. He supported multiple good causes (including the March of Dimes). He was honorary chairman of Fight for Sight, a nonprofit that funded research for vision-related problems. Just that year, he had received the S. Roger Horchow Award for Greatest Public Service by a Private Citizen, a prestigious national honor bestowed by the Jefferson Awards Foundation. (Walter Cronkite was the recipient the previous year.)

The Shannons With Bob Hope

But the causes couldn't all be trusted; some weren't legitimate. And Bob Hope wasn't about to jump into something without caution.

"I'll tell you what, if it's good enough for Marie and the Osmonds, it's good enough for me," he said to Joe as Marie stood next to him. "I'll give you my likeness and my image for a year and see how it works. But don't ask me to go anywhere and for any money."

Bob turned and said to Marie, "I'm in."

The deal was struck. Bob Hope's name went on our letterhead. Over time, the letterhead's value would prove to be negligible. We didn't wind up doing much with that kind of marketing. But the involvement of Bob Hope would prove to be the gift that kept on giving. One more valuable link in our growing chain of credibility. Much more than a famous name on a piece of stationery, he became a tireless and proud proponent of the Children's Miracle Network, never ceasing in his support, helping in countless ways. Just weeks after that first meeting, he allowed me to bring the Video West crew to his home in Toluca Lake to shoot a promo spot of him urging viewers to tune into the upcoming Children's Miracle Network telethon on May 29. Bob's backyard was a par three golf course, with an eight-foot wall all the way around his property. Because Bob's sight was failing, the cue cards were written with very big letters. It fell to me to pull the cue cards for Bob. At one point Bob said, "Where the hell did you find that kid pulling those cue cards? Can't you find somebody that knows what they're doing?"

Bob Hope was seventy-nine years old when he and Joe had that conversation in his dressing room. Twenty years later, ever the comedian, he sent Joe a note, which read: "Dear Joe, you're a hell of a salesman. I'm in the twentieth year of a one-year commitment."

He passed away a year later, just after his hundredth birthday; a great humanitarian and CMN friend who can never be replaced.

J. Gary Sheets, Chairman of the Board of Trustees, 1983-1985

....

CHAPTER FIFTEEN

Million Dollar Takeover

Two weeks before our first Children's Miracle Network telethon, on May 17, 1983, we held a Board of Trustees meeting. It took place in the conference room at the office building in downtown Salt Lake City where our Board chairman Gary Sheets ran his financial services business.

In addition to our eleven inaugural Board members, all of them local business people and community leaders, we invited a delegation from the National Association of Children's Hospitals and Related Institutions—NACHRI—to attend. They would be representing their forty-four children's hospitals to discuss the possibilities of developing a relationship with CMN . Weeks earlier, when I was in Colorado recruiting the Denver Children's Hospital (unsuccessfully, although they joined later), Stuart Turgil, the development officer at Denver Children's, suggested I give the folks at NACHRI a call. Until then, the only thing I knew about NACHRI was that it was the group that ran the convention in Chicago where we were able to recruit several hospitals that joined the network.

NACHRI was an organization that advocated for children's hospitals nationwide, working with state and federal governments and other entities to lobby for its member hospitals and make sure they got all the benefits and grants available to them. In 1983 NACHRI's membership of forty-four children's hospitals included many of the most elite children's childcare institutions in the country. For a new organization like ours, based entirely on servicing children's hospitals, it made sense to see what kind of relationship we could develop. NACHRI agreed. They sent their top executives to Salt Lake City for our Board meeting: Bob Sweeney, NACHRI president, and John Jeffries, CEO of Buffalo Children's Hospital and chairman of the NACHRI Board. Their attorney, Big John Hopkins of Atlanta, rounded out the delegation.

After a few preliminary items on the agenda, the CMN Board invited the NACHRI contingent into the conference room. Big John Hopkins, who stood six-foot-six and weighed about two sixty, took the floor. He was a commanding presence in all respects. He was a partner in King & Spaulding, a powerful Atlanta law firm that had recently sent another of its partners, Griffin Bell, to Washington as President Jimmy Carter's Attorney General. Big John got right to the point. NACHRI had done its homework on the Children's Miracle Network. They were impressed with the groundwork that had already been laid and could see great possibilities for the organization in the future. So impressed that they came with a very surprising, completely unexpected proposal.

Big John Hopkins offered Joe and me **$1 million**—$500,000 each—to turn over the network to them and go away. They had the documents all drafted, ready for our signatures. Big John put two checks down on the table for $50,000 each. NACHRI was offering Mick and Joe $50,000 each per year for the next ten years. When I left the March of Dimes I was making the most I'd ever made in my life, $35,000 a year. Hmmmmm.

This got the attention, needless to say, of not only Joe and me, but everyone in the room.

NACHRI wanted to take us over lock, stock and barrel, using their resources, experience, and expertise to really make something of what we had started. Big John explained that their intention was to keep the network exclusive by limiting it to their forty-four member hospitals. In their view, "daycare centers," like St. Luke's Hospital in Boise, should not be participating. Their assumption, based on their observations of our day-to-day operations, was that it was a two-man outfit run by Mick and Joe. A couple of cowboys from Utah.

Not so fast!

Now they found themselves looking not at Mick and Joe, but at an eleven-member Board of Trustees...that now had a decision to make.

As Board chairman, Gary Sheets did not hesitate in stepping forward to take control of the situation. He politely thanked Big John Hopkins and the NACHRI executives for their presentation, and asked if they would please give us the room so the Board could consider their proposal.

As they left the room, almost before the door could hit them in the butt on the way out, with no hesitation—and with Joe and me sitting there with our mouths open—Gary said, "We're not doing that!"

Gary next said, "All in favor?" And all eleven hands went up.

Joe and I were both left wondering, what had just happened? Fifty thousand dollars a year! (**YOU GOTTA BE KIDDING!**)

Gary had been with us from the beginning. He saw the big picture. He knew what we were working toward. Over the last year he'd witnessed the dedication and passion of everyone involved. He understood what we were trying to build—a nationwide children's hospital network that would help sick children anywhere and everywhere. Most important of all, he knew this was much bigger than Mick and Joe. "We have our whole team together and we owe it to everyone to stay with this and bring it along and build it up," he said. "We're not going to put the brakes on, we're not going to turn our backs and turn it over to somebody else and just walk away."

With very little discussion, the members of the Board all nodded in agreement.

Joe and I didn't know quite what to think. Needless to say, neither one of us had ever been offered a half-million dollars before. It wasn't like we couldn't use it. After fifteen months of no paychecks, we were hurting financially. Joe was completely tapped out. I still had a little cushion, but not much. But both of us knew Gary was right. He was saying what he should have said, speaking in the best interests of kids, not for the interests of any one person or any two people. It was the reason we had a Board of Trustees; it was why setting up a strong Board was the first thing we did when we incorporated. This would never be the Mick and Joe show; never had been, never would be, never could be. For any nonprofit to survive and thrive, a responsible Board needs to be fully in charge, guaranteeing trust and integrity and responsible decision-making—and that was especially true for this nonprofit that was hanging on by its fingernails.

The Board wasn't working for us. We weren't their bosses. We worked for them. We had no say in whether we should take the $1 million. That was the Board's call. Not ours.

Gary invited the NACHRI people back into the room. He thanked them for their offer and was diplomatic in declining to accept it. The Children's Miracle Network would remain its own separate entity, thank you very much, but if possible also wanted to establish a strong working relationship with NACHRI.

I'm sure Big John Hopkins, Bob Sweeney, and John Jeffries, in their wildest imaginings, hadn't expected to come to Salt Lake City and have their million dollars turned away flat. But now that Gary Sheets and the Board had their attention, everyone sat down to discuss ways we could interact and help one another. Bob Sweeney said NACHRI wanted to stay involved and asked to have representation on the Board. We agreed to allocate NACHRI seven seats on a new fifteen-member Board, still retaining an eight-seat majority for CMN. It was also agreed that in August, several weeks after the first telethon had been aired, the newly constituted Board would meet to get organized.

After we adjourned, Gary Sheets turned to Joe and me as we collected our papers.

"Come in guys, let's talk about this for a minute," he said, and motioned us into his office.

Gary looked across his desk at two guys who had in essence just been offered a half-million each for fifteen months work. He sat down and wrote out two checks. He handed one to each of us. Each check was for $25,000, drawn on Gary's personal account.

"Here's a little something to keep your families going," he said.

So…here we go…two weeks later our first telethon broadcast takes place, thanks to the following donations:

All talent fees donated. . . . . .Priceless

The Osmond family, Osmond Studios. $300,000

Brett Hutchens and Duff's restaurants. $150,000

Bill Marriott, free hotel rooms $100,000

Linda Dozier Western Airlines, free airfare $100,000

Bonneville Broadcasting satellite time . . . . $ 90,000

Bonneville Broadcast satellite uplink. $25,000

Gary Sheets (finally), a salary for Mick and Joe . . . . $ 50,000

Brighton Bank office space . . . . $ 25,000

(**YOU GOTTA BE KIDDING!**) $840,000

These truly amazing people and donations **MADE THE MIRACLE HAPPEN**. There would be no Children's Miracle Network today without them.

The Osmond Brothers treat their fans to some good old country charm.

....

CHAPTER SIXTEEN

Twenty-one Hours Live

Memorial Day Weekend, May 28-29, 1983: In many respects, the first Children's Miracle Network telethon looked very much like the March of Dimes telethons that preceded it. We had KSL-5's crew. We had ace producers Al Henderson and Mike Mischler. We had Bonneville International's satellite uplink and donated airtime. For the third year in a row, we had rent-free use of the state-of-the-art Osmond Studios—a donation of almost $1 million over the past three years.

But in other respects, the landscape had changed dramatically. We had grown to thirty TV markets now, representing twenty-two children's hospitals. And most significantly, in past years the existence of the organization did not hang on the success or failure of the telethon. Now it did.

We hoped the Memorial Day weekend would be a good time to draw in viewers, just as we hoped that the public would be as inclined to give to children's hospitals as to the March of Dimes, if not more. But we were a brand new charity in a new time slot with no tradition, no name recognition, and no parent company in New York to bail us out. No one knew for sure what would happen.

With the promise of a bigger national audience, Joe was successful in getting commitments from more top name performers. Joining co-hosts John Schneider, Marie Osmond, Merlin Olsen, Marilyn McCoo, and many more celebrities from the year before, the newcomers included magician David Copperfield; Howie Mandel, the TV doctor on *St. Elsewhere*; twelve-year-old Ricky Schroder, just off his role as Jon Voight's son in the movie, *The Champ*; Tom Wopat and James Best, better known as Luke Duke and Sheriff Rosco P. Coltrane on *The Dukes of Hazzard*; Dean Butler from *Little House on the Prairie*, and The Oak Ridge Boys, among others.

A big draw for the performers was the proven track record of the Osmond Studios and producers Al Henderson and Mike Mischler. The studio offered the best of everything—lighting, audio, wardrobe, sets, even a great green room. Everyone knew they would be performing in one of the top facilities in the world. Al and Mike brought with them their first-class crew. Audio producer Pete San Filipo (who would later produce the audio for *Seinfeld*), flew in from New York City. Dave Stoddart, lighting director for *Donny & Marie*, brought his expertise in orchestrating amazing light shows and grasping the emotions of the moment. Seven Nielson, set designer from *Donny & Marie*, was a genius at selecting and coordinating sets. Brent Fuelner had proven to be an extraordinary director. Denny Crocker, the Osmond's musical director, was in charge of the band. Entertainers could feel secure that they would perform in the best of conditions and get positive exposure for their careers.

Leading up to the event, there was some added drama when an organization called the Theatre Authority threatened to shut us down. The group's president, a woman named Yvonne Fairbourn, had reached out to us a few months earlier, asking us to meet with her in her Hollywood office. She explained that the Theatre Authority was a charity that funded a home for retired, indigent entertainers. She said the Theatre Authority was sanctioned by entertainment industry unions, and any charities utilizing any of the union's members must make a donation to Theatre Authority or the union would prohibit a celebrity's appearance. She insisted that the Screen Actors Guild and the Directors Guild backed Theatre Authority. She slipped a contract across the desk for our signature, requiring a payment of $300,000 or no celebrity would be allowed to perform at our telethon. This was no small threat, since Yvonne also told us that both Jerry Lewis and Easter Seals—the nation's largest telethons—paid the $300,000 fee.

It did occur to us that Jerry and Easter Seals were very big, and we were very tiny.

We hadn't encountered this issue in any of our earlier telethons so we began polling our entertainers to see what they knew about this Theatre Authority? No one had ever heard of them. The best we could determine was that it was an organization that raised money to help entertainers in their retirement years, a kind of pension fund for aging stars. Maybe that appealed to a segment of Jerry's performers, who were older, but our people weren't that old. We ignored the cease-and-desist demands from the Theatre Authority. We had no choice. We couldn't pay $300,000 because we didn't have $300,000. And even if we could, ain't no way. That money's going to the hospitals and the kids, where it was intended to go. As it turned out, we never heard from them again, not that year or ever. But it kept the suspense up right to when we went on the air. A year later, Hollywood was shocked when Yvonne Fairbourn was murdered in her kitchen.

To get all our entertainers from Los Angeles to Utah we again arranged for a charter flight to pick them up at the airport in Burbank. This time Western Airlines provided the plane, a 737. The goal was always to provide our celebrities with the utmost convenience and comfort. They were donating their time and talents absolutely free of charge and the best way to say thank-you was how they were treated. Board chairman Gary Sheets donated the use of his two jets, a Lear and a Citation, to get Joe and me and others on the CMN welcoming committee to

Burbank. We held a reception/party at the airport and then filled up the 737 with the entertainers and their friends and relatives and accompanied everyone back to Salt Lake.

At the Salt Lake Airport, a line of twenty Lincoln Town Cars stood on the tarmac, their trunks open with volunteer drivers ready to help the entertainers with their bags. They shuttled all of them to the recently opened Provo Marriott, our new headquarters hotel (thank you Bill Marriott) just a short drive from the Osmond Studios in Orem.

At nine o'clock Saturday evening the show began with the new Children's Miracle Network logo superimposed on the screen. The logo was designed by a direct-mail company in Nashville that was hoping to do business with us. We didn't end up doing much in the way of direct-mail advertising but they said the logo was ours to keep regardless. It was a hot-air balloon with a boy and girl riding in the basket. The design would change over the years, but the balloon would remain CMN's logo forevermore. Nike likes to brag that it paid an art student thirty-five dollars for its Swoosh logo. We did them one better. We didn't pay anything for our signature balloon logo.

Marie opened the twenty-one hours of live broadcasting with the Kool & the Gang hit song *Celebration*:

> *It's time to come together*
> *It's up to you*
> *What's your pleasure?*
> *Everyone around the world, come on!*

And on that note, after several months of sweating, planning, plotting, and uncertainty, we were up and running. When I die, we will play *Celebration* at my funeral.

Looking back at clips of that first show, I'm as proud today as I was then of the more than two hundred people who came together, the vast majority of them unpaid volunteers, to make it all happen. On stage, the four co-hosts, John, Marie, Merlin, and Marilyn, provided an incredible amount of energy. John sang *It's Now or Never*. Marilyn sang *Turn Your Love Around*.

Then Merlin set the tone for what it was all about when he introduced little six-year-old Danny Dyer to the audience. Danny was the first Miracle Child ever to appear on the Children's Miracle Network telethon. At the time, he was undergoing chemotherapy treatments at Vanderbilt Children's Hospital in Nashville for a rare form of brain cancer that had been discovered the previous year. Earlier radiation treatments had caused the cancer to disappear and now the hope was that the continuing rounds of chemotherapy would give Danny a clean bill of health.

Wearing a yellow shirt and a bald head due to the chemo, Danny melted everyone's hearts with his cheery, upbeat attitude. Danny came on stage with a guitar and sang a song his godfather had written for him to help him get through his ordeal:

David Hasslehoff holding Danny Dyer

Each day I get a little stronger Lord,
Each day I love you more.
Every day I'm learning Lord,
'Cause that's what life is for.
I've had my ups and I've had my downs,
And I've had my share of woes.
And I try again,
'Cause that's how a person grows.
I'm getting better and better every day I live,
And only let the good times show.
'Cause for every little drop of rain that falls,
Another flower grows.
I thank you Lord for all you've done.
Thanks for what you've given me.
Let me grow a little more each and every day
And think how strong I'll be.

Every hour we featured a miracle story. It became a staple that would be featured in every telethon that followed through the years. Nothing could tell who we were and what we were doing better than those amazing kids. We didn't exploit them, we celebrated them. We didn't feel sorry for them, we cheered them on. It was never, "If you don't give, these kids are going to die," but rather "Give and we are going to save lives!"

The pace backstage was frenetic. NACHRI brought several people to Orem to observe the show. One man we didn't know seemed to be roaming everywhere. We were about to ask him to leave when we found out he was Rand O'Donnell, the CEO of Arkansas Children's Hospital. We let him continue to roam. (A few years later he would be our third CMN chairman of the Board.) Another person hanging around backstage was Steve Young, the future Hall of Fame NFL quarterback. At the time, Steve was in his senior year at BYU. He had just signed the largest professional contract in the history of professional sports, $40 million, in 1983. Having done so, he had been booked to appear on *Good Morning America* and *The Today Show*. Coincidentally, he and I wound up on the same Western DC-10 flight from Kennedy back to Salt Lake. That DC-10 had seventeen passengers on it. Seeing Steve sitting on the other side of the plane and knowing him from my association with BYU football, I walked over and explained to him what we were doing with Children's Miracle Network. I told him that no matter where he ended up playing professionally, a children's hospital would be nearby and this was a cause he would want to be a part of. I invited him to come over to the Osmond Studios during the telethon and see what we were all about. As with Rand O'Donnell, it was the beginning of a beautiful relationship. Steve Young became a CMN fixture, never missing a telethon. For thirty-seven years he served as our national sports chairman.

It was a challenge while the telethon was airing live to contact our twenty-two hospitals' broadcasts being aired in various parts of the country and stay up-to-date on the funds they were raising. We'd call the telephone number for the station and more often than not get a busy signal. But despite the communication lapses, everything went off at the various locations even better than we dared hope. We had an interesting lineup of hosts at the regional remotes. In Arkansas, one of the co-hosts was the first lady of Arkansas—and later to become first lady of the United States—Hillary Clinton. Hillary and her husband Bill, then the Arkansas governor, were close friends with Rand O'Donnell, who made the arrangements for Hillary, who was on the Board of Arkansas Children's Hospital, to help with the telethon in Little Rock. It was the start of a lifetime of support for CMN from the Clintons that spread from Arkansas to the White House.

In Los Angeles, KHJ, the station airing the telethon, didn't have a studio, so it was up to Joe and I to both find a place to hold the regional telethon and the entertainers who would host the show. We found a studio we could rent from the local PBS station. For a host, a friend of Joe's, Steve Edwards, who did a morning TV show for the Los Angeles ABC affiliate, recommended a co-host of his, a former Miss South Dakota named Mary Hart. Mary, who had also just been tapped by CBS to host a new national show called *Entertainment Tonight*, agreed to host the L.A. local for us, and after watching tape of her from that first telethon, we could see why Edwards was so high on her. She was sensational. The next year, we requisitioned her to help host our national show. She became a loyal and longtime contributor to our telethons.

Brett Hutchens, the Duff's Smorgasbord president, had a significant presence on that inaugural telethon. We'd promised he would get plenty of air time and with Duff's being the (only) major sponsor he got it. We hung a sign at the back of the stage in a prominent position featuring the Duff's logo, the only visible sponsor designation besides a smaller Marriott Hotel logo we placed in front of the stage. Since there were few Duff's restaurants in any of the places we were broadcasting I'm not sure how much good it did, but Duff's got the exposure nonetheless, and like the rest of us, Brett soaked up all the positivity and good feelings that were always part and parcel of the telethon. In that very first telethon we established the model for corporate appearances and recognition that stands till today.

Near the end of the broadcast, Brett came on stage with John Schneider and said he had an announcement to make.

"Mick and Joe don't know this," he said as he took the microphone from John. "But Duff's would like to commit to provide $180,000 to cover production costs for year two."

Brett Hutchens makes a surprise announcement at end of 1983 show.

Joe and I were at the production table watching the monitors when this happened. Brett was right. We had no knowledge or warning whatsoever he was about to do such a thing. We were speechless. Our nagging concern was how we would be able to cover our costs and continue going forward. In one short pronouncement, spoken for the whole world to hear, we knew for the first time there would be a year two! (**YOU GOTTA BE KIDDING!**)

Anyone seeing millions of dollars being pledged during the telethon couldn't possibly appreciate why $180,000 was so important to the future of CMN any more than they could know who "Mick and Joe" were. But the millions in pledges couldn't go anywhere other than the children's hospitals to which they were committed. That was our 100 Percent Local promise. The money from Duff's meant we could continue to raise those millions that could only go to the kids.

Following that announcement, John was joined onstage by his three co-hosts, Marie, Merlin, and Marilyn, as six o'clock Sunday evening approached. They proceeded to thank anyone and everyone who had helped make the telethon a success. They singled out Bob Sweeney and John Jeffries of NACHRI, who had watched and taken notes during the broadcast. John quoted the poet Carl Sandburg: "'A baby is God's opinion the world should go on.' Well, through your generosity and your efforts, watching the show, helping the kids, we know that it's your opinion that our work here with the Children's Miracle Network Telethon should also go on. Thank you!"

"The world's a nicer place," said Marie.

"It wears a nicer face," said Merlin.

"Thanks to you," said Marilyn, who was joined by her husband, Billy Davis Jr., to sing their hit (and our unofficial anthem) *Up, Up and Away* as a finale. Balloons had been passed out to the members of the studio audience, who held them high as all the entertainers and the miracle kids came on stage to help Marilyn and Billy finish the song.

Then Merlin Olsen turned to the giant tote board at the back of the stage, which now showed this total: $4,760,444. (We think??)

"Four million, seven hundred sixty thousand dollars!" he proclaimed. "Thank you all, very, very much."

And that was a wrap. We had more than doubled what we had raised in any previous telethon.

The most talented crew you could ever imagine had made this happen, skilled people who made certain Children's Miracle

Network got off to a great start. All were recognized as the closing credits rolled:

Executive Producers: Mick Shannon, Joe Lake

Producer: Allan Henderson

Co-Producers: Virginia Schmidt, Steve Lowe

Associate Producers: Mike Reese, Terry Shaw, Paul Roden

Technical Supervisor: Dave Bird

Directors: Brent Fuelner, Harper Nelson, John Marsh

Audio Director: Pete San Filipo

Lighting Director: Dave Stoddard

Art Director: Seven Nielsen

Technical Directors: Reid Griffiths, Thom Grow

Production Coordinators: Donna Hamilton, Jane Jones

Assistant Directors: Steffny Fuelner, Patrice Sheffer

Stage Managers: Mark Shattuck, Steve Thompson, Ron Hansen

Videotape Coordinator: Ross Jones

Camera Operators: Lee Ollerton, Jim Sorensen, Jerry Ashby, Al Cutler, Scott Murphy, Russ Crabb, Steve Lyon, Marty Metcalf, Lee Byers, Evan Kirschner

Audio Mixers: Blaine Stewart, Jon Hollowman, Merrill Jenson, Tony Armstrong

Audio Stage Managers: Tony Simmons, Pete San Filipo, Jr., Less Udy, Charles Sisson

House Sound: Steve James, Phil Hodson

Audio Maintenance: Tom Nielsen

Audio Assistants: Chuck Criddle, Mark Miner, Donna Brighton, Heidi Parker

Video: Andy Carleton, Russ Merrill, Ron Ruiz

Video Maintenance: Jerry Huber, Dean Komatsu, Rick Lehtinen

Videotape Operators: Randy Lowder, Jeff Taylor, Mike Jex, Mike Russell

Assistant Lighting Director: Kurt Jurgens

Follow Spots: Paul Larson, Rhett Fernsten, Kevin Bernett, Mike Goodman

Set Decorator: Gary Riggs

Props: Susan Riggs, Don Sough, Rob Means, Lee Baird

Utility: Rick Josephson, Rick Chrisman, Wayne Walser, Keith Richens, Lynn Maughn, Carey Smith, Ross Rieman, Pam Phillips, LaRon Stevens, Doug Jensen, Mike Baird, Pete Hansen

As I always did, I bundled up the tapes of the show and took them home to watch immediately. I was quickly convinced this was our best effort yet. The years of experience showed, and more than that, there was a passion and determination that spread and gained momentum through the entire broadcast. By comparison, the Jerry Lewis MDA Labor Day Telethon, in its 17th year, raised $28 million that year. It was televised on more than two hundred stations throughout the nation. We managed to raise nearly $5 million, in our first year, on just thirty stations—and every last penny of that nearly $5 million was going to help kids. The Children's Miracle Network Telethon had struck a chord. Within three years we would pass Jerry Lewis, within five years we would more than double his total. But we didn't know that on Sunday afternoon, May 29, 1983. All we knew is we'd be around for at least one more year.

MIRACLE CHILDREN

Children's Miracle Network has always been and always will be about the kids. It is the **Why** behind everything that happens. **Putting Kids First** drives every fundraiser, every sponsor relationship, every decision. Each of the chapters that follow, as we chart the progress of CMN from fledgling startup to the world's most successful children's charity, will be preceded by a Miracle Child story.

MIRACLE CHILD

Baby Jessica

Outside of her family and a few friends she played with at the daycare center her Aunt Jamie ran out of her house in Midland, Texas, no one had ever heard of Jessica McClure on October 14, 1987.

Two days later, the whole world knew who "Baby Jessica" was.

In an unguarded moment, eighteen-month-old Jessica had crawled to a small well in her aunt's backyard and fell in, dropping all the way to the bottom, twenty-two feet below the surface. When her horrified mother, Cissy, who had gone inside to answer the phone, saw what had happened she ran back in the house and called the police, who were on the scene in three minutes flat.

But all they could do was stare down into the narrow hole and hear Jessica's whimpering. The diameter of the pipe the toddler had plunged into was just eight inches at the top, widening to fourteen inches at the bottom. The opening was barely big enough for someone as small as Baby Jessica to fit into. At the bottom of the hole she lay contorted—but still upright and able to breathe.

The police and the paramedics who joined them scratched their heads. They couldn't fit into the well and they couldn't remove the pipe to make the hole wider without endangering the child.

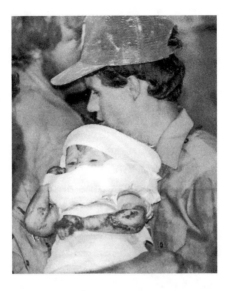

Rescue worker carries Jessica Mcclure
after rescue from well

Soon, a small army was huddled in Jamie Moore's backyard trying to figure out how to get to Baby Jessica. Midland is in the heart of west Texas oil country, so the army included a number of oil riggers who were experts at drilling wells. As they started devising their plans, they were joined by CNN's television cameras. The twenty-four-hour cable news channel that had been started seven years earlier by Ted Turner in Atlanta was still something of a novelty, its coverage hardly noticed alongside network giants ABC, CBS, and NBC. But here was a story tailor-made for CNN: a desperate round-the-clock struggle to rescue a young girl who had fallen down a narrow well.

Word spread as fast as the rescue effort went slow. The plan devised by the mining engineers was to dig a larger hole parallel to the one Baby Jessica was in and connect the two at the bottom with a horizontal shaft large enough for a rescue worker to be able to reach through and grab hold of the child. It looked great on paper, but the rock they had to bore into was harder than granite, and the sideways drilling presented challenges of its own. The work was painstakingly slow as the clock continued to click. Millions upon millions tuned into CNN for up-to-the-minute updates. At the White House, President Ronald Reagan was among those watching. "Everybody in America became godmothers and godfathers of Jessica," he said.

Finally, late in the day on October 16, as CNN filmed and America watched, a worker was able to reach through the gap between the two holes, reach in, and bring Baby Jessica to the surface. It had been fifty-eight hours since she fell into the well. The photograph taken by Scott Shaw of the *Odessa American* as she emerged from the ground in the arms of her rescuer won that year's Pulitzer Prize.

Rescue workers prepare to lower volunteer into a well parrallel to the one Jessica fell into

At the children's hospital, everyone was prepared for Baby Jessica. The CMN-member children's unit rushed her into surgery to remove a toe that had developed gangrene from loss of circulation. It was the first of fifteen surgeries the child would undergo for various complications from the ordeal. She had a steep hill to climb to recovery.

But she was a fighter, and after thirty-two days Baby Jessica was able to leave the hospital in time to spend Thanksgiving with her family.

The following year, we brought Jessica McClure and her parents to Disneyland for our CMN telethon as a featured Miracle Child—a healthy two-year-old who represented all that was good about courage and teamwork and the indomitable human spirit...and who needed no introduction.

Board of Trustees with their buddies, Mickey and Minnie

....

CHAPTER SEVENTEEN

They Only Had to Tell Me Once

Now that our first telethon was in the books, the first order of business was to meet with our newly constituted Board of Trustees and determine how we could best move forward.

As had been ably demonstrated at our pre-telethon meeting in May, the Board was in charge of the Children's Miracle Network, period. Not Mick and Joe. Not the salespeople. Not corporate sponsors. The Board of Trustees had complete and total control. It was one of our key founding principles—to be governed with absolute transparency and integrity. Honesty is important to all businesses, but especially so in the nonprofit sector. A non-paid, objective Board *had* to be in charge. Joe and I had to be accountable always.

In May we had agreed with NACHRI to provide the organization representation on the Board of Trustees. It was decided that the fifteen-member Board would be comprised of four hospital CEOs, two physicians, two hospital development officers, and seven at-large members. The makeup of the Board allowed for varying points of view from the CEOs who ran the hospitals, the development directors who were on the front lines of fundraising and public relations, the doctors who knew firsthand the needs of pediatric healthcare, and representatives of our sponsors who would bring with them a wealth of real world business experience.

The four hospital CEOs on the reconfigured Board that met in Salt Lake City in August of 1983 included Rand O'Donnell from Arkansas Children's Hospital in Little Rock, Blair Sadler from the Children's Hospital in San Diego, Stephen Perry from the Children's Hospital of the King's Daughters in Norfolk, Virginia, and David Gowing of the Children's Hospital of Eastern Ontario in Ottawa, Canada. The two physicians included Dr. Joseph Butterfield from the Children's Hospital of Denver and Dr. Richard Rapkin of the Children's Hospital of New Jersey. The two development officers were Norman Myers of the Children's Hospital of Columbus, Ohio, and Tom Sullivan of the Children's Hospital of Buffalo, New York.

At-large members included Gary Sheets as chairman; Brett Hutchens of Duff's Smorgasbord; Todd Clist of Marriott Corporation; Harris Cooper, CEO of Dairy Queen International; John Jeffries of NACHRI; Art Anderson, an accountant from Salt Lake City; and Alan Tibbitts of Brighton Bank of Salt Lake City. Sheets and Tibbitts were the only holdovers from the inaugural Board.

It was obvious from the get-go that these people were not part of any voting block. They were independent thinkers and always put the hospitals and kids first. It was in their DNA. It was their nature.

The top item up for discussion was criteria for membership in Children's Miracle Network. The NACHRI officers wanted the network to be comprised exclusively of the forty-four top-of-the-line children's hospitals that were NACHRI members. They were very open and up front about not wanting these elite hospitals to associate with places that didn't care exclusively for children or abide by NACHRI's strict standards. "Daycare centers," as they called them.

No one could begrudge the NACHRI members and their supporters for looking out for their members' best interests. It's what they did. It was why they offered $1 million to acquire the telethon three months earlier. They could see great potential for their member hospitals being part of a fundraising network. But they wanted it to be an elite, private club.

To the point of view of the rest of us, they were missing the big picture. For one thing, it was hard to see how the telethon could thrive long term, or even survive at all, by broadcasting in just forty-four markets. For another—and this was the most salient point—restricting membership wasn't in the best interest of kids. With a truly nationwide network—and that was our goal—we could be a much more powerful force in supporting children's hospitals. National sponsors would not be incentivized to participate if only a few of their locations were involved. Critical mass would be required.

Dr. Joe Butterfield, a NACHRI appointee and chairman of pediatrics at the University of Colorado medical school and chairman of pediatrics at Children's Hospital of Denver who was one of the two physicians on the Board, pointed out that restricting membership to NACHRI hospitals would cut out, for starters, all the great teaching hospitals on college campuses in America—including Duke, Vanderbilt, Johns Hopkins, USC, and so forth. He noted that the University of New Mexico Medical Center, a hospital that had been one of the twenty-two pioneers that participated in the first telethon, wasn't a NACHRI member. But UNM did far more for kids than Carrie Tingley, the small ten-bed hospital in Albuquerque that was a NACHRI member.

NACHRI president Bob Sweeney, who wasn't a Board member but was participating in the discussion, spoke up and insisted that Carrie Tingley, as a NACHRI affiliate, should be a CMN member ahead of UNM. He added that he had just talked to the Carrie Tingley CEO at his home, who told him his hospital wanted in.

That comment perplexed Joe and I. Earlier in the year, when we were signing up hospitals, we had met with the Carrie Tingley CEO and he told us he wasn't interested.

When the Board meeting, which was scheduled for two days, adjourned for the evening, Joe called the Carrie Tingley CEO at his home. His wife said he was out of town, attending a conference in Phoenix. When Joe reached him in his hotel, the CEO said he had never talked to Bob Sweeney. It seemed the NACHRI president had conveniently stretched the truth trying to make his case.

When Joe reported this at the next day's Board meeting, Bob Sweeney went silent, and suddenly the Albuquerque point was moot. UNM was in and Carrie Tingley, which was never in, was out. And Dr. Joseph Butterfield, who had said he'd resign if Carrie Tingley was chosen over UNM "because it wasn't in the best interest of the kids," remained a strong advocate on the Board.

In the end, an agreement was reached all could live with regarding NACHRI's position. It was decided that NACHRI members would have right of first refusal in their respective markets, to be secured by a $1,000 binder fee. Beyond that, CMN would continue to recruit hospitals throughout the country that were not children exclusive—such as St. Luke's in Boise—one hospital per market, also charging $1,000 binder fees to reserve the market. (In addition to the $1,000, each hospital's annual participation fee—to cover overhead and operating expenses—would be based on the size of its television market).

So the Board passed its first test unscathed. This was the Children's Miracle Network Board, dedicated to the best interest of kids. Period. Regardless of CMN or NACHRI affiliation, the Board established the precedent that kids came first.

The two-day meeting ended in consensus and solidarity, verifying the value of having a wide range of points of view and establishing a tradition of strong Board oversight that would be CMN's trademark. Throughout the years, these exceptional people consistently kept us on the straight and narrow, but always with a real world perspective. I remember one early meeting, when the Board was considering what level of spending I, as CEO, should be authorized to execute without Board approval.

Board member Harris Cooper, president and CEO of Dairy Queen International, our second big national sponsor, spoke up. He said, "If you can't trust him with $50,000, fire him!"

Within five years, the Board of Trustees was complemented by another powerful group: the Board of Governors. The idea for the Board of Governors came from Diane Doniger, who was Chairman of the Board at the University of Rochester Children's Hospital in Rochester, New York, and an at-large member on the CMN Board of Trustees. We were trying to open doors to corporate sponsors and Diane suggested putting together a collection of prominent people who through their connections and influence could help open the doors for us. Diane understood better than most the power of influential people. Her father was Don Regan, who had served as President Ronald Reagan's chief of staff. Her choice to head the Board of Governors was a man of great influence and integrity: Joe Viviano, president and Chairman of the Board of Hershey Chocolate and a previous member of the CMN Board of Trustees.

When Diane asked him to head the new Board, Joe laughed and said immediately, "If I'm going to do this we're going to get Don Soderquist and Drayton McLane too." Soderquist was COO of Walmart and McLane was CEO of the McLane Company that supplied goods and products to thousands of convenience stores nationwide. Soderquist and McLane were Hershey's two biggest customers. Thus the first CMN Board of Governors began with three absolute giants of American industry—men whose reach and influence would pay unbelievable dividends for CMN. When Joe Viviano, Don

Soderquist, and Drayden McLane called, people took the call. (**You Gotta Be Kidding!**)

The inaugural thirteen-person Board of Governors, in addition to Joe Viviano, Diane Doniger, Don Soderquist, and Drayton McLane, included Todd Clist of Marriott, Gary Crocker of Research Industries, Gene D'Angelo of WBNS-TV in Columbus, William Egan of Johnson & Johnson, Edward Horner of the Children's Memorial Foundation, Robert Rauscher of Amoco Oil, C. Frank Roberts of the *New York Times* Broadcasting Group, Donald Regan (Diane's father) of Regdon Associates, and Brett Hutchens of the Hutchens Company, who had just stepped down as chairman of the CMN Board of Trustees.

Diane's idea was genius. Meeting separate from the Board of Trustees, the Board of Governors would prove invaluable in bringing in a constant flow of new ideas and sponsors for CMN. On barely a moment's notice, someone in this group could get a meeting with anybody in the country!

Over the years, numerous titans of industry and commerce have stepped up to serve on the Board of Governors. One of them was none other than Mike Mischler, the man who teamed with Al Henderson to produce our first CMN Telethon at the Osmond Studios in 1983, and before that the acclaimed March of Dimes telethons. Al stayed on at KSL-TV in Salt Lake City, eventually becoming general manager. Mike took his talents to Hollywood, where he advanced through the ranks until he became senior vice president of marketing for CBS Television. Among other productions and career accomplishments, he marketed the *Dr. Phil Show* as well as *Wheel of Fortune* and *JEOPARDY!*—two of the longest-running game shows in the history of television. Always loyal to CMN, Mike was appointed to the Board of Governors thirty years after putting CMN on the map with his expertly-produced telethons, and eventually became Chairman of the Board.

To show our appreciation for the extraordinary efforts and sacrifices made by the men and women who selflessly served on the Board—they received no compensation and paid for their own travel (Marriott always took care of the lodging)—we at CMN management always tried to say thank-you by making a Board meeting trip a pleasurable experience. The first few Board meetings were held in Salt Lake City, but with trustees coming from all over the country, we could hold the meetings anywhere. One year we met in Manhattan, where the Board stayed at the Marriott Marquis in Times Square and saw John Schneider perform on Broadway in *Grand Hotel*. Another year in Toronto they saw Donny Osmond in *Joseph and the Amazing Technicolor Dreamcoat*. In Los Angeles we arranged to take the Board to *The Tonight Show*. Another year we held our Board meeting at the PGA headquarters in Jacksonville, Florida, where the Board members were able to golf at the vaunted stadium course at TPC Sawgrass. Another year, for our national celebration meeting, with 1,100 attendees, Disney closed Disneyland and turned the park over to us. It took planning to make these trips happen, but it was important to let the Board know how valuable they were to the organization. They deserved to be treated as such.

At our annual conventions, we invited speakers like Mike Krzyzewski, Drayton McLane, Stephen R. Covey, Dr. Phil, Don Soderquist, and Richard Paul Evans. All were very powerful keynoters.

When people ask what the secret sauce is to the success of Children's Miracle Network, my answer is always: The Board. The strong, unwavering Board. And there was nothing secret about it. The governance, leadership, and mentoring of the Board was everything. I learned so much, in so many ways, from these people. **THEY ONLY HAD TO TELL ME ONCE!**

Maranda Francisco

Merlin Olsen recalled a bubbly five-year-old from the 1987 telethon. "Maranda, just wanted to dance. And she did just that as she danced her way through our hearts. She was just darling."

It was a miracle that Maranda Francisco, from Denver Colorado, was able to express her joy in dance. She couldn't always express anything in such a lively manner. Very early after birth her young body was restricted by Rasmussen's Encephalitis, a rare inflammation of the brain tissue with no known cure. At eighteen months she had her first epileptic seizure. This was the first in a series of long and frequent seizures that would continue unabated for over two years. Twitching would begin in the right corner of her mouth and would gradually spread, affecting only the right side of her body. The convulsions became more frequent, often occurring 120 times a day at intervals of three to four minutes. Seizures often interrupted her in mid sentence of in between bites of food. Her life was a succession of occasional episodes of relative calm between convulsions. Falling asleep was her only escape from this tormentor.

After extensive testing doctors found that the left hemisphere of Maranda's brain, the portion that is responsible for speech and the functioning of the right side of the body, was swollen and would eventually cause paralysis, possible mental retardation, or even loss of life. The only way to stop the seizures would be radical brain surgery. The doctors would have to remove the left hemisphere of her brain, hoping the seizures would stop.

Doctors felt that because Maranda was still young, chances were good that the brain's right hemisphere would compensate for the loss of the left one. At the age of four Miranda was flown from **Denver Children's Hospital** to **Johns Hopkins Children's Hospital** in Baltimore to undergo the extensive ten-hour surgery. World renowned pediatric neurosurgeon Dr. Benjamin Carson was to perform the surgery. Yes, the same Dr. Carson that ran for President in 2016.

"My philosophy is to look at a patient and ask what is the worst that could happen if we do something?" he explained. "It is usually that the patient ends up seriously debilitated for dead." Then I ask, "What is the worst that could happen if we do nothing?" and it is usually the same thing. So with that background, I figure it's always worth trying to do something, if there's any chance that doing something might end up helping."

Maranda Francisco danced her way into
our hearts

In a crowded operating room at Johns Hopkins Children's Center Dr. Carson drilled six holes the size of shirt buttons in Miranda Francisco's skull. Those holes formed a semi circle, beginning in front of her left ear, curving up across her temple, above one ear and down behind her other ear. With an air-powered saw, Carson connected the holes into an incision, and folded back the left side of Maranda's skull, "like you would a book" to expose the outer covering of her brain. He injected a drug to reduce the swelling, inserted a tube to drain some of the excess fluid and remove the hard outer covering of the brain.

"That leaves the brain surface staring at you," he said. "It was tense, swollen, and angry looking." Miranda lost nearly nine pints of blood during the operation. By the end of the procedure, Carson and his surgical team knew they had successfully removed the left hemisphere of Maranda's brain. What they didn't know was whether the seizures would stop and whether she would even talk or walk again. In the recovery room Terry Francisco, Maranda's mother, bent down and kissed her daughter, not knowing if she would respond or not. "

When a groggy Maranda finally opened her eyes in the recovery room and said, "I love you, Mommy and Daddy," Terry Francisco completely lost it, as did everyone else in the room. " I was totally ... well, talk about tears of joy!" Maranda's mother said.

Less than a year later, Maranda was the picture of health at the 1986 Children's Miracle Network Telethon when she came on stage to get a big hug and to be interviewed by Merlin Olsen.

A nationwide television audience was inspired by her Miracle Story of resilience and recovery—and none to a greater degree than a young mother watching the show in Cleveland.

Anne McCameron was sitting in a Cleveland clinic with her four-year-old daughter Jennie. Like Maranda, Jennie was born with Rasmussen's Encephalitis. Her story paralleled Maranda's almost to a T: fine till two years old, then the seizures began, until she was having more than one hundred a day and had to eat through a tube to stay alive. Jennie's doctors had recommended the radical brain surgery to Anne and told her about a young girl from Denver who had come through the operation successfully.

Now, on Memorial Day Weekend, Anne McCameron wiped tears away as she watched that girl from Denver cavort around the stage on the Children's Miracle Network Telethon.

Anne had been struggling mightily trying to decide if Jennie should have the brain surgery. "Just the thought of cutting open her head and taking out half her brain was terrifying," she said. "But then I saw Maranda, with her little curly hair, laughing and clapping. It had to be fate. I told myself, 'this is meant to be.'"

A few short weeks later, Jennie McCameron went to Johns Hopkins and had the same surgery as Maranda Francisco—with the same miraculous result.

Gary Sheets

....

CHAPTER EIGHTEEN

Deadly Packages

Two men. Two leaders of Children's Miracle Network. Two tragedies.

I knew GARY SHEETS and TOM MOSSER as men of principle, with hearts of gold, who thought of others first. Gary was the first chairman of the CMN Board of Trustees. Tom served on the Board of Governors. Each dedicated countless selfless hours to the cause of saving the lives of children. That death and evil-doing should invade their worlds was as cruel as it was unexpected. To make it even worse, each was victimized by his own success.

Gary Sheets didn't die at the hands of a bomber, but his wife, Kathy, did—by opening a package that was addressed to Gary. Kathy's killer was a forger named Mark Hofmann. The bomb he delivered to the Sheets' home was a diversion, meant to throw suspicion away from his crimes.

Kathy Sheets was the second person killed the morning of Oct. 15, 1985. The first was Steve Christensen, a young man who until recently had worked with Gary Sheets at his Salt Lake City finance company, Coordinated Financial Services. As in any investment venture, some people make money and some people lose money—leaving some disgruntled investors. Hofmann knew this. In a separate relationship, he and Christensen were negotiating a deal for Hofmann to sell to Christensen what he purported to be rare documents relating to the early history of The Church of Jesus Christ of Latter-day Saints. A devout Mormon, Christensen was eager to get the documents so he could donate them to the church. But Hofmann was having trouble coming up with the documents he claimed to have and was concerned Christensen was close to uncovering his fraud. He placed a pipe bomb outside the door to Christensen's office at 6:30 a.m. Three hours later, after Christensen picked up the bomb and died, Hofmann placed a second bomb at the Sheets residence so the police would think the bombs were related to CFS's financial woes, apparently sent by angry investors.

And that's exactly what the police did think initially, until the following day when Hofmann inadvertently set off another bomb in his car, nearly killing himself in the process and bringing all the attention on him. Several months later Hofmann agreed to a plea deal, avoiding the death penalty by confessing to the two murders and his forgeries. Of the death of Kathy Sheets, Hofmann callously said, "At the time I made the bomb, my thoughts were that it didn't matter if it was Mrs. Sheets, a child, a dog…whoever."

Mark Hofmann was sentenced to life in prison without parole.

At the time of his wife's death, Gary was about to finish the final year of his three-year term as Children's Miracle Network Board Chairman. Everyone at CMN was devastated for him. I was in the office when the news of the bombing came on the radio. I drove to his home to see what support I could offer, but the police had sealed off the area and we couldn't get close. Gary had done wonders for CMN in those beginning years. He stared down NACHRI when they offered us $1 million to sell out. He flew our telethon guests here, there, and everywhere in his company's jets, asking for nothing in return. He reached into his own pocket many times to keep us going, including writing the $25,000 personal checks he gave to Joe and me when we hadn't been paid for months. He was a warm, friendly, engaging person. He always had time for you. He had his ups and downs in business. When his company floundered the government charged him with fifty-two counts of fraud. He had to deal with that right after the death of his wife. He went to court and was found not guilty on all fifty-two counts. Part of the government's case involved CMN. One of our first hires was Jay Vestal, a sharp development officer at Arkansas Children's Hospital who had caught our attention. We talked Jay into coming to Salt Lake City as our first professional development officer. We couldn't afford to match what Jay was making at Arkansas Children's, but we were able to make it work by letting him live in a condominium Gary Sheets owned in Salt Lake. The FBI believed we were paying Gary under the table for the use of his condo so he wouldn't have to pay taxes. The truth was, Gary donated the condo with no strings attached. Jay and his family stayed there for free.

Later in his life, we were able to properly honor Gary Sheets at our national meetings in Orlando, recognizing him as the first Chairman of the Board and honoring him with the Founders Award. His leadership and vision were absolutely critical for Children's Miracle Network to survive and thrive.

Gary died in 2018 at the age of 84. I went to his funeral in St. George, Utah. It was a huge gathering. I was surprised when the family asked me to come up and say a few words about my friend. I retold the story about the $25,000 check, and how he'd kept alive an organization that was broke when he took over and by the time of his death had contributed $7 billion to children's hospitals.

In his obituary, it was stated: "Gary had a knack of making you feel like you could accomplish anything in life, and would remind you of your greatness often. He was free with compliments, stingy with criticism, generous with a smile, and always the eternal optimist. One of his proudest achievements was serving as the founding chairman of the Children's Miracle Network, an experience he mentioned often toward the end of his life."

Thomas J. Mosser was a self-made star in the advertising and public relations business. He graduated from St. Bonaventure University in New York with a bachelor's degree in journalism and worked briefly as a reporter for the Associated Press before joining the U.S. Navy and serving as an officer in Vietnam. After the war he took a position with the elite public relations firm Burson-Marsteller when he was twenty-five years old. He was general manager of the firm's New York office at thirty-nine and at forty-five was named president of its Americas division, in charge of public relations for major accounts such as AT&T, Coca-Cola and, unfortunately as it turned out, Exxon Oil. In the early '90s, as he was promoted to executive vice president of Young & Rubicam, the ad agency that was Burson-Marsteller's parent company, he was recruited to join our Board of Governors and bring his expertise and connections to CMN.

Tom was about to go out with his family to buy a Christmas tree on Dec. 10, 1994, a Saturday, when he sat down at the kitchen table to open a small package the size of a videocassette that had arrived in the mail the previous day. The package was a bomb. It exploded on contact, tearing a hole in the kitchen counter, breaking out windows, spreading smoke through the house, and instantly ending Tom Mosser's life.

Tom was murdered by the notorious UNABOMBER, the reclusive anti-technology terrorist who was caught by the FBI sixteen months later. For eighteen years, from 1978 through 1996, Ted Kaczynski, aka the Unabomber, killed three people and injured twenty-three with his bombs. Tom Mosser was his second-to-last victim. Tom was fifty years old. He was targeted because the public relations firm he worked for, Burson-Marsteller, handled the account for Exxon. This was right at the time of the Exxon-Valdez oil spill. As Kaczynski wrote in his confession in the *New York Times*, "We blew up Thomas Mosser last December because he was a Burston(sic)-Marsteller executive." Ironically, Mosser had left Burson-Marsteller and was in fact working for Young & Rubicam, the parent company, when he was killed. Like all his other victims, the Unabomber did not know Mosser. He was merely a symbol.

The tragedy hit the CMN family hard. Tom Mosser was praised universally for his kind nature and good works. "The closest thing to a Boy Scout you're going to find in business today," said the CEO of Burson-Marsteller, James Dowling. At St. Bonaventure, his alma mater, an outpouring of support from friends, alumni, and associates endowed the Tom Mosser Scholarship, an annual award that continues to this day.

MIRACLE CHILD:

ANDREA EDORIA

Mary Lou Retton and Kerri Strug are all smiles on the cover of the summer 1997 issue of *Miracles*, the magazine of the Children's Miracle Network, as they embrace seven-year-old Andrea Edoria. The two gold-medal Olympic gymnasts know all about overcoming injury to reach their full potential—and so does little Andrea.

Andrea was born with a birth defect that affected the proper formation of arteries and veins at the base of her brain. For the first three and a half years of her life she displayed no symptoms that anything was wrong, but all the while the blood vessels near the top of her spinal cord were weakening and growing into a tangled mess. In the middle of the summer of 1996, just after attending ballet lessons, Andrea suffered a stroke.

At first her pediatrician thought she had the flu and sent her home with orders to drink soup and stay in bed. But as she watched TV, Andrea said to her mother, Evita Valero, "Mama, how come I can see two TVs?" Whatever she had, it definitely was not the flu. She was rushed from her home in Pasadena to

Children's Hospital Los Angeles, where Dr. Gordon McComb, chief of neurosurgery, prepared for surgery. As she lie in her bed, Andrea, an avid dancer, was able to watch the gymnastics competition at the 1996 summer Olympics In Atlanta, where Kerri Strug would dramatically clinch gold for the U.S. team.

The surgery to identify and cauterize the arterial venous malformation took eleven hours. When it was over, Andrea could not speak, swallow, chew, sit, walk, or even hold her head up. She was starting over.

Mary Lou Retton and Kerri Strug surround Miracle Child, Andrea Edoria

With the fortitude of youth she began again. Within five days she was doing physical, occupational, and speech therapy every day. Doctors were wary of placing any kind of timetable, or guarantee, of Andrea's recovery. But like Mary Lou, who needed serious knee surgery just six weeks before she competed as an Olympian in 1984, and like Kerri, who had to produce her final vault to secure gold for the U.S. team on a badly twisted left ankle, she persevered and triumphed. Four months after surgery she was able to leave the hospital and continue her therapies at home.

By the time she was seven, a fully-recovered Andrea was back taking her dancing lessons and selected as that year's CMN Champion from California. That in turn led to her "photo shoot" with the two Olympic gymnasts and CMN ambassadors, Mary Lou and Kerri, who congratulated Andrea with huge hugs, recognizing a champion when they saw one.

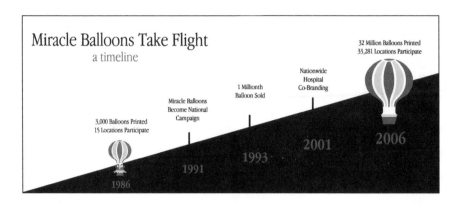

Miracle Balloons Take Flight
a timeline

3,000 Balloons Printed
15 Locations Participate

Miracle Balloons
Become National
Campaign

1 Millionth
Balloon Sold

Nationwide
Hospital
Co-Branding

32 Million Balloons Printed
33,281 Locations Participate

1986
1991
1993
2001
2006

Top national brands teamed with CMN to bring about a steady rise in donations

160

....

CHAPTER NINETEEN

Cause Marketing

Every year we managed to exceed the total raised for children's hospitals, from the $4.7 million announced at the telethon in 1983 to $13 million in 1984 to $22 million in 1985 to $30 million in 1986. More and more television stations and children's hospitals joined each year, bringing with them more and more viewers who contributed more and more donations.

But phone pledges on telethon weekend were only part of it. A big share of the early growth in revenue came from a yearly $5 million deal Jay Vestal, our new chief development officer, negotiated. Having $5 million already on the books before the telethon began was the definition of a good start.

Jay was originally from Dallas, but he came to us by way of Arkansas and he brought with him an understated southern charm. Jay was the kind of person who always under-promised and over-delivered; the direct opposite of the stereotypical used car salesman. When he walked in the room he didn't overwhelm anybody; he was all substance and integrity.

Jay had met with an advertising executive named Bill Lembeck, who connected him with News Corporation, the international mass media conglomerate owned by Rupert Murdoch. As part of its business, News Corp printed what were known as Free Standing Inserts, or FSI's: advertising fliers that would go inside millions of newspapers nationwide.

The FSI's typically were themed around major holidays or events—Super Bowls, Mothers Day, Easter, Christmas, Thanksgiving, World Series. They served the dual purpose of publicizing the event and advertising a company's products. In the early to middle 1980s, thanks to an executive named Jerry Welsh, more and more of these FSI's were themed around charitable causes.

In 1983, the year CMN came into being, Welsh had come up with a model he called cause-related marketing, or Cause Marketing for short. It all stemmed from the Statue of Liberty needing a facelift for its 200th birthday party coming up in 1986. Welsh was executive vice president of communications and marketing for the American Express Company. As fate had it, his office window in downtown Manhattan looked directly at the Statue of Liberty in New York Harbor. The statue's condition had been neglected for years and was badly in need of repair, as Welsh could clearly see looking out his office window. Welsh saw a win-win situation. What if American Express came up with a campaign to refurbish the Statue of Liberty and Ellis Island in time for its bicentennial? It would be support for an undeniably good cause while at the same time generate tremendous publicity for the company.

For the final three months of 1983, American Express announced it would donate to the Statue of Liberty renovation one cent for each credit card transaction and one dollar for each new credit card account opened. Besides being heavily advertised and marketed by American Express, the campaign wound up attracting a tremendous amount of free publicity in newspapers and magazines, and on television and radio. At the end of the three months, Welsh had his win-win: $1.7 million had been raised for the refurbishment and American Express card usage had risen by twenty-eight percent. Cause Marketing was born. Over the next three years, twenty-one companies joined American Express in the effort to clean up the Statue (And increase their exposure and their profits.) Together these companies raised $69 million for the facelift and untold billions in revenue increases for themselves. By the time of the centennial celebration in 1986, the Statue of Liberty and Ellis Island looked as good as new.

Buoyed by their success, Welsh and American Express went so far as to copyright the term "Cause-related Marketing."

We invited Jerry Welsh to one of our early CMN Board meetings, held in Manhattan, to learn more about the intricacies of Cause Marketing. He spent the afternoon with us at the Times Square Marriott Marquis.

"The wave of the future isn't checkbook philanthropy," he told us. "It's a marriage of corporate marketing and social responsibility."

Capitalizing on this new trend of Cause Marketing, Jay Vestal and Bill Lembeck were able to secure twenty top national brands that wanted to associate with Children's Miracle Network in a Free Standing Insert campaign. The group included such giants of American commerce as Hershey's, Post Cereal, Coca-Cola, Heinz Ketchup, Campbell's Soup, Kodak, Sara Lee, and Johnson & Johnson, among others.

The cover of the insert, which was distributed in newspapers in early May, told all about children's hospitals and was a major promotion for the telethon coming up on Memorial Day weekend. Inside, each sponsor expressed support for CMN along with special promotional offers and clip-out coupons. The twenty companies paid $250,000 each to CMN for a total of $5 million. The companies were then featured during the telethon, bringing added value to their themed FSI. (CMN member hospitals each received a portion of the $5 million based on the percentage of the total TV households in the country they represented.)

The FSI's went on for more than a decade and were a huge boon to CMN in the critical early years. Not only did it mean a consistent infusion of funds and associate us with strong, reputable products and companies, but it publicized who we were and what we did via literally millions of inserts distributed to households in every corner of the country. (As an added bonus, Paul Carlucci, the News Corp executive who negotiated the deal, became a strong believer in and supporter of CMN, later joining the Board of Governors. Carlucci was publisher of the *New York Post* and had a considerable amount of influence in New York City, the number one market in the country. Upon his retirement, Carlucci was recognized by receiving the Founders Award at CMN's annual celebration meeting.)

In the meantime, we were doing everything we could to keep the lights in the office on. Our promise that "100 percent stays local" did not allow us to take a portion of the $5 million that came from FSI sales, or any other funds collected specifically for the hospitals, for operational expenses. **100 PERCENT LOCAL** was a founding principle we would not budge from. No other charity had such a model. All collected a percentage of what they raised for administrative needs. Refusing to do that set us apart. It made us unique. It put kids first unequivocally. If you donated a dollar to your children's hospital through CMN you could rest assured the entire dollar, every last cent, would wind up at your children's hospital. None of it would pay someone's salary or go into somebody's expense account. This gave us integrity.

It also gave us a difficult bottom line. We were constantly looking for ways to take care of the overhead and maintain the office and pay the salaries of the staff. About eighty percent of those expenses were covered by the annual fees paid directly to CMN by our member hospitals, but we made every effort to keep those fees as low as possible. To make up the difference, we developed some stand-alone events in an attempt to generate revenue. Early on, we did an Osmond family concert in Boise and another in Omaha to raise needed funds. But we were always looking for more ways to raise money to operate.

Some of my ideas were spectacular. Some were duds. None lacked enthusiasm and energy. One of the early ideas Joe and I came up with was the M*A*S*H Bash. As anyone who was alive in the 1970s and 1980s knows, M*A*S*H was must-see TV. The comedy series about a mobile army hospital in the Korean War ran on television for eleven years, from 1972 to 1983, and was one of the most-watched television shows in history. The series finale was viewed by 106 million people, still an all-time record for a single TV episode.

Our idea was to piggyback the biggest TV event in history. We just had to take advantage of this. We recruited the services of KSL-TV, as they had every episode of M*A*S*H in their library, and made an unprecedented hour-long tape of M*A*S*H highlights. To air the tape publicly, we discovered that the Actors Guild, the Directors Guild, and every star whose image would be used in the tape, had to give their written approval. Undaunted, Joe went to Hollywood, spent a week on the Fox lot, and achieved the impossible. He convinced each star of the show to give him a letter authorizing our use of their image on the tape. Then he went to the Directors Guild, and only because he had everyone's signature, they agreed to grant their permission. After that he went to the Actors Guild, and they agreed too. Several of the show's stars agreed to come to Utah for the event, including William Christopher (Father Mulcahy), David Ogden Stiers (Major Charles Emerson Winchester III), and Gary Burghoff (Radar).

We had become aware that the Mormon Church "owned" several days every year at the Salt Palace Convention Center in Salt Lake, so we went to the Presiding Bishop's office at LDS Church headquarters to see if they would be willing to donate to us the Saturday night before the Sunday night final episode of M*A*S*H. We were aware the church donated some of their days to the Boy Scouts, and felt a children's charity might also qualify for their service. Without deliberation, they gave us the date.

We sent a highlight tape to a number of the hospitals in our network, about twenty-two of them in all, along with a how-to book with details about how to put on the event in their area. All were to be held on that Saturday night.

The night of the party 2,800 people showed up at the Salt Palace in Salt Lake, all dressed up like their favorite M*A*S*H character. The crowd would vote on the best Clinger, the best Hot Lips, the best Father Mulcahay, and so forth. Everyone came ready to party. M*A*S*H definitely had a lot of fans. One of our interns had managed to secure the donation of some pizzas. The truck backed up to the door and plugged in twelve little plug-in pizza ovens. The ovens would cook a pizza in twelve minutes. Each pizza was six slices. That meant we could cook 360 slices an hour. Do the math. It would take eight hours to cook enough pizzas for the 2,800 people! Still, everyone had a great time. To this day, people don't remember the lack of food, they remember a great M*A*S*H Bash. We ended up raising just over $16,000 in Salt Lake, considerably below our expectations. However, at the time, $16,000 was a very big deal, and in all, the twenty-two M*A*S*H Bashes around the country generated just under $300,000, capital that was sorely needed at the time to keep the lights on and the office solvent.

One of the more *brilliant* ideas I had, we called Dance Across America. Here the concept was to have dance parties at locations all across the country, with the participating dancers raising money through pledges, in a format similar to a walkathon. We partnered with a national scholastic organization called DECA— Distributive Education Clubs of America—to reach the teenagers who would be critical to the fundraiser's success. We asked Andy Gibb of the BeeGees to serve as national chairman of Dance Across America and took him with us to the DECA national convention in San Francisco to secure them as our partner. DECA clubs at high schools throughout the country agreed to host dance parties that would be linked by closed circuit via KSL's satellite, creating a huge Dance Across America party. In

Utah, we used a roller rink, Classic Family Fun Center, donated by one of our volunteers in the Salt Lake suburb of Sandy to hold our dance party. Then...nobody came. We didn't have a hundred people at our event in Sandy, and half of them were our own kids. It was the same story at the fifty or so locations around the country. It was on us for poor organizing and execution of the event. We lost $100,000. It almost put us under. We were good at what we were good at, oops!, and not so good at what we weren't good at.

Believe me, I could write a whole 'nother book of dumb ideas I had like this.

But we managed to learn from our mistakes. Over time, we became more inventive, coming up with just enough private underwritings to keep us afloat. We did things like adding a sponsored Miracle Child segment to each telethon, underwritten by sponsors who knew of our operational needs. Out of necessity, we kept the office staff small—up until 2010 it never grew to more than fifty people. It was never about how many we had, but rather how few we had. Financial responsibility had its virtues. It kept us lean and hungry and kept our focus on the reason we were in business—to raise money for the hospitals and the kids.

Still, our biggest and most constant worry was generating enough support to keep us viable and secure. The FSI's were a great asset. But how long would they last? And what would replace them when the time came?

After Gary Sheets stepped down as chairman of the Board of Trustees when his three years were up at the end of 1985, Brett Hutchens was elected to take his place. We could not have asked for a more enthusiastic, capable leader. Since day one, Brett had been our most ardent supporter. As president of Duff's Smorgasbord, he had made sure the production costs of the first two telethons were funded. When Duff's was acquired by outside investors in 1984, Brett formed his own real estate development company. In his new business, he had come in contact with a company he thought might be a good fit for CMN.

Brett said to Joe and I: "What about Walmart as a sponsor?" And Joe and I said: "Who?"

Tangela Roberts

By the time the twenty-first century was underway, bone marrow transplants had become the accepted procedure to cure a blood disorder called sickle cell disease. But to show that the approach was viable back in 1991, it took a team of innovative oncologists at the Medical University of South Carolina Children's Hospital...

...and a brave little girl named Tangela Roberts.

Sickle cell disease, also called sickle cell anemia, is an inherited blood disorder most commonly found in people of African descent. The disease is characterized by abnormal red blood cells shaped like sickles that inhibit the flow of oxygen through blood vessels, resulting in tissue and organ damage. Over the long term, vital organs, including lungs, liver, spleen, and kidneys, shut down.

In the short term, those afflicted with the disease experience what are called "pain crises," with bone discomfort so debilitating that morphine and other strong painkillers are required, and often hospitalization.

For Tangela Roberts, her pain crises began in the womb. Her mother, Angel Roberts, experienced such difficulty during pregnancy that she was hospitalized on numerous occasions— all because of her unborn daughter's sickle cell disease. After Tangela was born, she almost immediately began suffering. Hers was a particularly acute case. She spent weeks at a time in the hospital. By the age of three and a half, doctors were running out of ways to help her. That's when Dr. Miguel R. Abboud, a pediatric hematologist/oncologist at **MUSC Children's Hospital** in Charleston, South Carolina, suggested a bone marrow transplant. The theory was that replacing healthy stem cells from a donor's marrow for the faulty stem cells in Tangela's marrow would end her pain and allow her to live a normal life.

But it was unquestionably risky. At the time, bone marrow transplants were being done in other areas of medicine, but not yet for sickle cell disease. The surgery would be experimental. No one knew for sure if it would work.

There could be complications, as Tangela's immune system would be completely shut down during the process when chemotherapy treatments would completely destroy her own bone marrow. Tangela's parents, Angel and her husband Paul, weighed the possibilities and the dangers as the doctors gave them time to make their decision.

After much praying and agonizing, the Roberts' gave Dr. Abboud and his team the green light. Tangela's seven-year-old brother, Paul, Jr., was found to be a perfect match and agreed to donate his healthy bone marrow. It meant a few days in the hospital for recovery for Paul, but he did not hesitate to help his little sister.

After the surgery, Tangela remained in isolation while doctors continually checked her blood to see if the transplant was working. After five weeks everyone was satisfied. Her immune system was up and running and her blood work was perfectly normal. Not a sickle cell to be seen. Most importantly, free from pain, Tangela was laughing and singing and her body was growing.

"It was as if she had emerged from her own secret world of misery," said Dr. Sherron Jackson, a member of the transplant team.

Tangela was the first person in the United States to have a bone marrow transplant for sickle cell disease. Thanks to her pluck and spirit, and the dedication of a pioneering group of doctors at a Children's Miracle Network hospital in South Carolina, it wouldn't be the last.

Mick, Donny Osmond, Sam Walton and Joe

....

CHAPTER TWENTY

Fifteen Minutes that Changed the World

In his commercial real estate development business, Brett Hutchens had developed a relationship with Walmart, helping them acquire land and build new stores, which they were doing at a prodigious rate in 1985. The discount merchandiser was already a huge presence in the southeast and midwest sections of the country, with 882 stores in nineteen states. The company was already well on its way to becoming the largest retailer and employer in the world (In 2019 Walmart had 11,000 stores in all fifty states and twenty-eight countries, employing 2.3 million people).

But in 1985 there were no stores yet in the West (Utah wouldn't get its first Walmart until 1990). So when Brett first mentioned Walmart to Joe and me, we barely reacted. It wasn't as if he'd said IBM or General Motors.

A short time after that, Brett was on a business trip with Rob Walton, the head of the Walmart real estate committee and the son of Walmart founder Sam Walton. They were at an airport in Kentucky when a rainstorm delayed their flight. To pass the time, Brett pulled out a letter Joe and I had recently sent him.

"What you got there Brett?" Rob asked.

"Just a letter," Brett answered.

"Well what's it about?"

"It's a charity I got involved with."

Rob asked him to tell him a little more about it. By the time they were ready to board their flight, Rob was intrigued. He said to Brett, "Why don't you write me a letter and tell me more about this charity."

Brett went back to the office and wrote a five-page letter explaining CMN and the work it did with children's hospitals. He sent it to Rob. After Rob read the letter, he called Brett and asked him if he'd come to Walmart headquarters in Bentonville, Arkansas, for a meeting with his father and other Walmart executives to talk more about Children's Miracle Network.

Brett immediately called out reinforcements. He telephoned Marie Osmond and asked her to meet him in Nashville and they'd go to Bentonville and tell the CMN story together.

"It was very informal," Brett remembers of that meeting. "There were about six of us sitting around a little table. Marie and I met with the Waltons and David Glass, Don Shinkle, and Don Soderquist."

Informal or not, the wheels were set in motion. A year or so later Don Shinkle asked if Joe and I would be able to come to Bentonville for one of their weekly team manager meetings. Every Saturday morning, district and regional managers for Walmart would meet at Walmart headquarters—near the little Five and Dime store Sam Walton opened in downtown Bentonville in 1962 to begin the empire—to review the week's business activity and discuss strategies.

We were invited on a Saturday when Walmart was participating in a golf-and-tennis fundraising event for a cause supported by the supermarket chain Food 4 Less. The event was being held at the Bella Vista Country Club near Walmart headquarters. We brought reinforcements too. Donny Osmond agreed to participate in the fundraiser as a tennis partner with Sam Walton. Joe, Donny, and I flew to Fayetteville, the nearest commercial airport to Bentonville, and met Brett. The four of us made our way to Bentonville to get ready for the next morning's team manager meeting, which started at seven o'clock sharp.

More than four hundred district and regional managers filled every seat in the Walmart auditorium. Watching the attention to detail was fascinating. They knew every pack of gum they sold that week. There's a ramp that runs down the middle of the auditorium where everyone makes their presentation. Sam walked up the ramp and said he'd been to a store in Texas the week before, went in to get some shotgun shells, and they didn't have any.

"Who's got that store?" he asked.

"That would be me, Mr. Sam," said the unfortunate manager.

"Get some shotgun shells in that store."

Sam told the story of a store that had over hired and had to lay off twenty people. "Do you know what that does in a small town, letting twenty people go like that?" he said. "Making mistakes like that, we just can't do it."

Then he told the story of a developer in Birmingham, Alabama, they were working with to build several new stores. "They don't have a jet, these are our kind of people," said Sam.

I got the distinct impression the Walmart culture was not developed to drive business, it was developed to drive the right way to go about business. At one point everyone in the room did the Walmart cheer. This was back when the logo continued a line in the middle—Wal-Mart—that they called a squiggly. The cheer went: *Give me a W, give me an A, give me an L, give me a squiggly, give me an M, give me an A, give me an R, give me a T. What's that spell?*

In my mind I was ready to shout, WAL-MART. But everyone in the room shouted, "THE CUSTOMER COMES FIRST!" To a Walmart manager, that was what Walmart spelled.

I was given five minutes toward the end of the meeting to make our presentation. I thought about something the executive vice president of marketing for Sara Lee had once

told me: "If you can't sell it in seven minutes you can't sell it."
Five minutes was close enough. We showed the Alvaro Garza
video, a beautiful and dramatic retelling of the eleven-year-old
North Dakota boy whose life was saved at St. Luke's Children's
Hospital in Fargo after he spent forty-five minutes under the
water in a frozen North Dakota river. That took three minutes.
There wasn't a dry eye in the room when it was over. In the
remaining two minutes I emphasized that 100 percent of all
monies donated stayed with the local hospital where it was
raised. When I sat down we got a standing ovation. The Garza
film, as it always did, had hit its mark.

Afterward, Joe drove Donny to the tennis club and Brett got
in his car to play golf in the fundraiser. That left me standing
with Sam Walton. The founder of Walmart invited me to ride
with him the fifteen miles to Bella Vista. I got in Sam's pickup
truck, a seven-year-old dented up Ford F-150 with red-and-
white stripes that today has a prominent place in the Walmart
Museum. The truck fit the owner. Once, when asked why
he drove a pickup, Sam answered, "What am I supposed to
drive my dogs around in, a Rolls-Royce?" There was nothing
pretentious about Sam Walton. He was wearing Keds, jeans,
and a long-sleeved work shirt. His dog usually rode shotgun,
but out of deference to me I got the passenger seat and the dog
rode in the back. Sam wore a Walmart ballcap. He'd handed
one to me as well when we exited the company meeting. It still
sits in a prominent place in my home.

He talked in an informal manner as we drove. He talked
about the fondness he and Walmart had for Arkansas Children's
Hospital. He reiterated what he'd heard at the meeting:

"Now everything we do is going to stay local, right? he said.

"Yes sir, 100 percent stays local. We don't touch it, we don't
see it," I said. "Our business model allows fundraising to go
straight to the local hospital."

"So this is going to benefit our people where they live."

He chewed on that for a minute. Then, as he turned into the clubhouse parking lot, Sam Walton turned to me and said the five words that **changed everything:**

"OUR PEOPLE WILL AMAZE YOU."

With that, he got out of the truck. There were no lawyers, no contracts involved, not even a handshake. But it was clear Walmart was joining the CMN cause, and it was its associates—they're never employees, always associates—that would amaze the world. It was clear Sam Walton loved and respected those associates.

Sam went off to play tennis with Donny Osmond (four of the skinniest legs you'll ever see), while Brett went off to play golf at the country club. When they were finished, Joe, Brett, Donny, and I had a late lunch with several Walmart people. By this point Joe, Donny, and I had missed our flight out of Fayetteville. We drove down a dirt road to the little Bentonville Airport. There was a single man working in the shed. He asked if he could help us. We said, "We don't know. But we're stuck and we need to get to Kansas City." He said he would fly us there for $600. From there we were able to catch a connecting flight to Salt Lake City, capping off a long, rewarding, momentous, and historic day.

I had time on the plane to think about what Sam was telling us in those five words, **OUR PEOPLE WILL AMAZE YOU.** I realized that what he was saying is that Walmart would support children's hospitals, but it would not be through a traditional corporate contribution. No one from Walmart headquarters was going to write a check. Rather, they would **empower** the associates and customers in their hundreds of stores to use their resources and standing in their communities to fundraise for their local children's hospitals—through raffles, bake sales, car washes, canisters next to the cash register, the paper balloon icon program, and whatever else they came up with, all with the affirmation and support of Walmart leadership. Every penny collected would go to the local children's hospital that was as much a part of the community as they were. Properly run and motivated, it had the potential for far more buy-in and support than a marketing department coordinating the effort, or an executive sitting down and writing a check. This was people power!

We had already been doing something along those lines with Dairy Queen. A year and a half earlier, in 1984, Debbie Neer, the CMN director at Gillette Children's Hospital in Minneapolis, called and said she thought we ought to talk to Dairy Queen about a corporate sponsorship. (Debbie's husband worked for Dairy Queen). I flew to Minneapolis, Dairy Queen's headquarters, and met with Gary See, the vice president of marketing. Gary quickly sized up what we were trying to accomplish and saw that it was a great cause and fit for the company to get behind.

"We're in," he said as we shook hands, followed by, "We'll figure this out."

What they figured out was that the best way for Dairy Queen to participate was to have their individual franchisees and stores do the fundraising. Dairy Queen corporate would offer its endorsement and support, but the money would come from the grassroots level through the individual DQ operators, who would be free to choose their own ways to raise money.

This led to a lot of inventive fundraising campaigns, be it something as basic as a canister on the counter, to a bake sale, to donating a percentage of a day's or a week's or a month's sales to the local children's hospital. At the 1986 telethon, after only a few months of fundraising, Dairy Queen presented a check to John Schneider that reflected the combined nickels, quarters and dollars hundreds of Dairy Queen franchises had collected that went directly to their local children's hospitals.

In essence, that's what Sam Walton had committed Walmart to do at the end of our fifteen-minute ride. Instead of corporate giving coming from the few who sat in the executive tower, it would come from all the people who *were* the company.

It was a concept that would do nothing less than change the world of philanthropy and charitable giving.

The first thing we did after we returned from Bentonville was begin to develop a model for that type of campaign. We worked with Don Shinkle, Walmart's director of communications, to come up with a fundraising guide to send to Walmart's hundreds of stores. We had a model for corporate franchisee locations, and we had a model for corporate-operated locations. The revolution sparked by five simple words had begun!

Best of all, it was a model that could fit everybody. As Marriott was about to find out.

Just weeks after talking to Walmart, Joe and I flew to the headquarters of Marriott Hotels in Bethesda, Maryland, outside Washington, D.C. For three years, as Marriott had generously supported us with hotel rooms, we had developed a relationship with Steve Weisz, Marriott's vice president of marketing. Steve had agreed to meet with us to talk about Marriott increasing its participation as a corporate sponsor. Anticipating our visit, Steve was waiting with good news. Marriott was not only going to continue to provide us with rooms, but they also had a check made out to Children's Miracle Network for $300,000.

We thanked Steve for the contribution and then told him we had something else in mind for the next year.

Joe and I explained the Workplace Fundraising model being used at Walmart and Dairy Queen. We suggested that Marriott could tailor its own version of this model. We called it Marriott Pride and presented a fundraising guide to him. It made perfect sense for the company. Almost every children's hospital in America had a Marriott hotel nearby, often several Marriott hotels. What better cause for the people at those hotels to get behind than providing direct support to the hospital down the street? And what better cause for the Marriott brand to associate with? With the $300,000 we'd been offered for the next year, we advised that Marriott might consider hiring a fulltime person to supervise the program and coordinate with CMN for direction and campaign materials.

This is how Steve Weisz told the story:

"Mick and Joe came in and said, 'We've got a different idea. We don't want you to write a check any more.'

"I said, What! What!"

"They went on to explain the notion of engaging the people who worked for our company, and also associating with our guests, to raise money for Children's Miracle Network. I realized they had just come from Walmart and were excited about how this was all going to work."

By the time the calendar ushered in 1987, few skeptics remained, and fewer still after the 1987 telethon—when Don Shinkle of Walmart walked to center stage and made a check presentation on behalf of Walmart associates everywhere. The check, representing less than a year's fundraising by Walmart associates, was for $2.1 million. We knew Walmart had been busy, we had no idea they'd been that busy. It was by far the largest single check received to that point by Children's Miracle Network, and just the beginning of the more than $1 billion Walmart's amazing people would raise over the next thirty-five years. **YOU GOTTA BE KIDDING!**

APARICIO FOGG

"Y'all look for a miracle around here, because that's what you're gonna get." So stated Gailtricia Fogg, whose seven-year-old son, Aparicio, lie in a coma in the intensive care unit at **The Children's Hospital** in Macon, Georgia.

Ten days earlier, a healthy, happy, energetic Aparicio was at the bus stop waiting to go to school when a car struck him, fracturing his skull. He was rushed to The Children's Hospital, an affiliate of The Medical Center of Central Georgia, where a CT scan showed massive head trauma and serious swelling. As doctors sprang to action to try and stabilize Aparicio, who was bleeding from his nose, mouth, and ears, the prevailing feeling among the medical staff was that he'd likely not make it through the night.

When he did make it through the night, the prognosis still was not bright, with anti-swelling efforts showing limited success. After ten days, with Aparicio still in a coma, doctors met with Gailtricia and her husband, Tracy, who worked as a payroll administrator at the hospital. Their son had a thirty percent chance of ever regaining consciousness, they were told, and if he did wake up, he had a sixty percent chance of having severe brain damage. The chance he'd recover to resume his normal life: just ten percent.

That's when Gailtricia Fogg cleared her throat and gave her miracle prognosis. "We understand what you're saying, and you all have been just wonderful," she said. "We know you have to tell us what's in the medical books and what you know. But we're telling you that he is going to be fine."

Mom was right.

It wasn't easy. But after three weeks in the ICU Aparicio started breathing on his own and the ventilator was turned off. He was transferred to **Scottish Rite Children's Hospital** in Atlanta for physical, occupational, speech, and recreation rehabilitation therapy. After two months he was discharged for continued therapy at home. He had hearing loss in one ear, and speech and gait impairment, but by his ninth birthday he was out of his wheelchair and walking again, with more progress projected for the future.

As soon as he was able, he became an ambassador for the children's hospital fundraisers in his hometown. As a Miracle Child, he met and posed for a photograph with San Francisco 49ers Super Bowl-winning quarterback—and longtime CMN supporter— Steve Young, who said, "When the unthinkable occurs, it takes great inner strength and spirituality to get through trying times."

Thirty Years together

....

CHAPTER TWENTY-ONE

Workplace Fundraising: The New World

W orkplace Fundraising—that's the phrase that best described Our People Will Amaze You.

Raising money in this manner was an entirely new way of doing business in the nonprofit world. No one had ever done this. United Way used a form of Workplace Fundraising by having a company's employees participate in payroll deductions, regularly donating a portion of their paycheck. But fundraising campaigns that were employee- and customer-driven and directed, with corporate approval, were nothing short of revolutionary. It gave people at ground level the freedom to exercise their creativity and come up with marketing strategies and ideas that were truly grass roots.

People like Eleanor Lancey.

Eleanor was the Children's Miracle Network coordinator at Newington Children's Hospital in Newington, Connecticut (later Connecticut Children's Medical Center). One day in 1986 she received in the mail a marketing packet from CMN headquarters that contained materials with our ubiquitous balloon graphic. A light went on for Eleanor. What if she made an enlarged version of the balloon and used it as a way for businesses to raise funds?

She designed an orange- and yellow-colored balloon about the size of an eight-by-ten sheet of paper, added the CMN logo, and printed hundreds of the balloons on the hospital copy machine. She then went around to businesses in Newington and surrounding towns, suggesting they pass these out to their employees and customers. Anyone who made a donation to the Children's Miracle Network could write their name on the balloon and hang it on the wall.

O'Rourke's Diner, a restaurant in nearby Middletown, Connecticut, was the first business to sign on to Eleanor's campaign.

Mick, Eleanor Lancey, and John

When Eleanor returned two weeks later to see how it was going, owner Brian O'Rourke proudly pointed to more than 2,000 balloons on the wall—$2,000 raised, a dollar at a time. The names on the balloons were from customers and employees alike. People of all ages and walks of life had responded to supporting Newington Children's Hospital. Their names were up there on the wall for all the world to see. Soon, other area businesses joined the effort. The balloons provided a visible way for people to connect to a local treasure. The campaign was a runaway hit.

It became obvious that this could be replicated throughout the CMN network. Here was a campaign that could be used at all sponsors and businesses, no matter the size, from the local bar to Walmart. Before long, hospital coordinators were delivering miracle balloons to businesses across America. We contracted with a company in Price, Utah, Pezcuh Printing, to print and ship the balloons. Millions of them were going out every month. Eleanor became known as the Balloon Lady. By the 1990s her balloons were consistently raising in the neighborhood of $30 million a year. (**YOU GOTTA BE KIDDING!**)

A vast and impressive array of Workplace Fundraising campaigns were developed. At Marriott, Keith Kocarek, vice president of customer advocacy at Marriott Vacation Club International, had the idea to sponsor a walk between a Marriott Hotel in suburban Virginia and the Children's National Medical Center in the heart of Washington, D.C. The fundraiser proved so successful that soon it was being replicated in other parts of the country. Eventually those original twenty-five miles morphed into the Torch Relay for Children's Miracle Network, a Marriott-sponsored 5,000-mile cross-country event that wound its way through twenty-eight cities in eighteen states, connecting Marriott properties from Chicago to Los Angeles and attracting 2,500 participants who raised millions in pledges.

That event was put together by Steve Weisz's son, the first time in thirty-seven years where support of CMN was passed on to the next generation.

In Dairy Queen lore, there's the story of Sam Temperato, aka "The Father of the Blizzard." In 1984, the same year Dairy Queen International made the decision to partner with CMN, Sam and his brother invented a machine that could instantly make a mixed frozen ice cream treat the brothers called a "Blizzard." The next year, Dairy Queen sold 175 million Blizzards. Sam, who owned dozens of Dairy Queen stores in the St. Louis area, decided to make a contribution to CMN for every Blizzard sold at his stores during a certain time period—a simple, straightforward campaign that became a yearly tradition.

In 2006, Dairy Queen International formalized Sam's Blizzard idea into Miracle Treat Day, a one-day fundraising campaign for all DQ locations in North America. No one caught the spirit of the event more than DeLon Mork, the owner of the single Dairy Queen franchise in Madison, South Dakota. DeLon had recently watched his father die after a battle with cancer and the experience had caused him to become more in tune with the suffering of others, especially children. That first year, DeLon's franchise sold 3,083 Blizzards on Miracle Treat Day. And he was just getting started. The next year he sold 7,011 Blizzards, the most of any Dairy Queen franchise in North America. Every year he set a goal to top the record of the year before. He started a tradition of jumping out of an airplane when each year's goal was met. One year the governor of South Dakota jumped with him, another year the chief of police. Miracle Treat Day became a community celebration in Madison. Year after year, DeLon surpassed the previous year's total, until 2014 when he sold 47,638 Blizzards, still the one-day single-store DQ record, and one that may never be broken. All this, in a small town in the southeast part of South Dakota. Through 2018 Delon's franchise had sold close to 300,000 Blizzards on Miracle Treat Day.

"Our team just loves working with Children's Miracle Network," said DeLon Mork. "We know 100 percent of what we raise goes to Sanford Children's Hospital in Sioux Falls. The entire community all 7,000 people gets behind our effort. The campaign has become a community tradition."

The Children's Miracle Network-Dairy Queen partnership has produced many dividends and memorable moments throughout the years, some expected, some unexpected.

Mick meeting with President Bush in the Rose Garden

Steve Young with
a Miracle Child

C-1

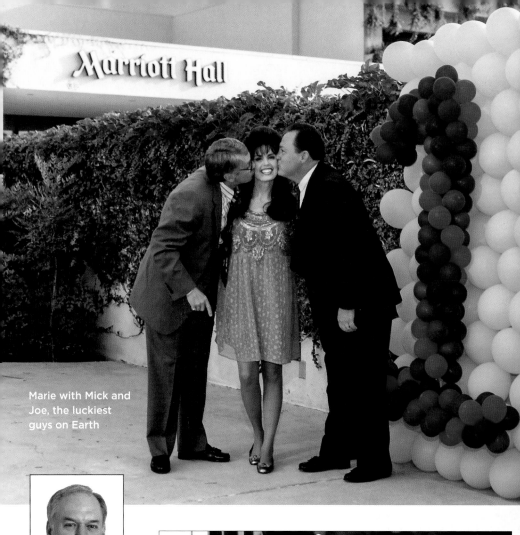

Marie with Mick and Joe, the luckiest guys on Earth

Stephen P. Weisz, Mariott Corporation—first national sponsor of the Children's Miracle Network.

Mike Reagan, REMAX and board member

John Schneider gets
a quick guitar lesson
from 1988 Miracle Child
Natasha Harris of
St. Louis.

John and Marie
visiting patients at
St. Rose Dominican
Children's Hospital
Las Vegas, Nevada

Bob Hope, Honorary
Chairman makes a
surprise visit to the
National Telethon.
With him are Marilyn
McCoo, John Schneider,
Marie Osmond and
Merlin Olsen.

$172,153,992

Above: Steve Young, Joe Lake, John Schneider, Marie Osmond, Mick Shannon, Robin Roberts, Mary Lou Retton and Merlin Olsen

Mick Shannon and Joe Lake, together with past Osmond Foundation Board Chairman, Brett Hutchens

Mick and Joe with Diane Doniger, founder of the Board of Governors

Our Partners
PUT THE MONEY
WHERE THE MIRACLES ARE.

Thanks to all of our partners, we raised more than
$360 million last year for children's hospitals.

 Children's Miracle Network Hospitals

cmnhospitals.org

2017 Edition of Best Hospitals
in U.S. News & World Report

Mick with NFL Commissioner Paul Tagliabue

Jon Vice, former board chairman

NFL Quarterback Club — Randall Cunningham
(Philadelphia Eagles), Jim Kelly (Buffalo Bills), Phil
Simms (New York Giants), Dan Marino (Miami Dolphins)

Walmart Associates — Over $1,000,000

Merlin Olsen, Marilyn McCoo, Marie Osmond, and John Schneider—
first Children's Miracle Network Telethon in 1983 at the Osmond Studios

Mick with 7-year-old Miracle Child Jayne Preucil of Omaha

Farewell to a Legend

"It has been a privilege to work so closely with Mick Shannon and help build Children's Miracle Network to what it is today. Mick's inspiration, dedication, and creativity have taken Children's Miracle Network to heights that none of us could have ever imagined"

Marie Osmond
Co-founder

Twenty-three years ago, Mick Shannon had a vision—a vision of an organization that brought together corporate sponsors, celebrities, television and radio stations, and other partners to raise money for children's hospitals. Little did he realize that his vision would exceed all expectations and that the organization he founded, along with Joe Lake, Marie Osmond and John Schneider, would blossom into one of the most influential, revered children's charities in North America. "When this all started, I simply believed that individuals could make a difference and I still do." It was Mick's individual passion that led Children's Miracle Network to where it is today—a major force for good in raising funds for 170 premier children's hospitals. As Shannon enters retirement he does so with fond memories and a firm conviction that the organization will continue to exceed expectations and touch even more lives. "There is no doubt in my mind that I have been the luckiest guy in the world," he said. "To meet the people I have met and to see the level of compassion out there is just amazing. I look forward to this organization continuing to grow and doing so much more than has already been done in the past."

"Being a part of this network of good that Mick Shannon has created is an honor for me, but also a great blessing for millions of kids throughout North America. Mick is not only a leader, he's a friend, an inspiration and a hero."

John Schneider
Co-founder

Marilyn McCoo, Mick Shannon, Brett Hutchens, Joe Lake, Mary Hart, Rich Little, Marie Osmond, John Schneider, Merlin Olsen

In 2002, I happened to be in Dallas for a CMN fundraising event with the Children's Medical Center of Dallas. Basketball star Shawn Bradley, the seven-foot-six starting center for the Dallas Mavericks, was one of our volunteer celebrities for the gala. While I was in town, Shawn arranged for me to meet Mark Cuban, the colorful, outspoken billionaire owner of the Mavericks.

A few weeks earlier, Cuban had made headlines when the National Basketball Association fined him for comments he made criticizing the refereeing. Cuban had said of Ed T. Rush, the director of NBA officials: "I wouldn't hire him to manage a Dairy Queen."

This, of course, did not endear Cuban to the people who managed Dairy Queens. From DQ's corporate headquarters in Minneapolis came this response:

"We are certainly impressed that Dairy Queen is top of mind with Mark Cuban. We like the publicity he's generated for us. But Mr. Cuban may be surprised to find out how much it takes to manage a Dairy Queen. We invite Mr. Cuban to manage a Dairy Queen for a day."

"Actually I would love to do it for a day," Cuban responded on ESPN. "I brought up DQ because I love 'em. Any additional pounds I have are due exclusively to Blizzards and Blizzards alone."

Arrangements were made for Cuban to "manage" the Dairy Queen in Coppell, Texas, just outside Dallas.

He served a few self-serve cones during his time at the store, which lasted about an hour, but he spent most of the time signing autographs. Our logo was front and center and received extensive publicity as local and national media covered the story. At the end of the day, that single Dairy Queen had raised $5,000 for CMN and we had gained a friend and priceless exposure. In parting, Cuban couldn't resist a final shot: he said the people who ran the NBA could learn a lot from the man who managed that Dairy Queen.

Marriott, Dairy Queen, Walmart…thanks to Workplace Fundraising the list of corporate sponsors continued to grow. More often than not, it was personal connections and relationships that made it happen. Such was the case when Stephanie Melemis, who was vice president of our CMN Canada operations, suggested we talk to RE/MAX, the huge international real estate company with franchises throughout North America. She set up a meeting for me with a friend of hers in Montreal who happened to be the largest RE/MAX franchisee in the world. That led to a meeting at RE/MAX headquarters in Denver, the city where Dave Liniger and his wife Gail created in 1973 what would become the largest real estate company in the world.

I met with Daryl "Jess" Jesperson, senior executive for RE/MAX (it stands for **RealEstateMAX**imums). I came prepared with a detailed presentation spelling out all the reasons Children's Miracle Network and RE/MAX was a good fit. Real estate agents are independent by nature, as well as natural born salespeople, and here was a perfect opportunity for them to create their own fundraising campaigns for their local children's hospital while at the same time drawing attention to RE/MAX and showing that this was a business that cared about the communities it served.

I was just getting started when Jesperson held up his hand. He got the concept of Workplace Fundraising almost before the words were out of my mouth. As I was talking he'd already done the math in his head, calculating the possibilities.

He said, "Let's say 70,000 agents, a hundred dollars an agent, we'll do seven million dollars."

He walked me down the hall to Gail Liniger's office, popped his head in to introduce me, and said, "We're going to raise seven million dollars for children's hospitals!" and walked out. And Gail didn't bat an eye.

From the start, everyone at RE/MAX was all-in. The born salespeople exceeded all expectations. Leading the way was Richard Phillips in Houston, owner of several RE/MAX franchises in Texas. It was Phillips who embraced the idea of the Miracle Home program, a campaign where every agent who sold a home would donate one-hundred-dollars to CMN from the sale. Every year Richard would sponsor a big fundraiser in Fort Worth at Gilley's, the famous Texas honkytonk. He'd have an auction, invite all kinds of celebrities, and throw a Texas-sized party.

From coast to coast, RE/MAX agents embraced Workplace Fundraising with amazing dedication and ingenuity. As pie-in-the-sky ambitious as Jesperson's original estimate might have appeared, at that it was right on the mark. In its first twenty-five years of sponsorship RE/MAX would contribute $157 million to Children's Miracle Network—an average of nearly $7 million every year!

The fact that the RE/MAX logo was a balloon, same as CMN, made the fit even more of a natural.

"The partnership was built on not just writing a check from corporate, because anybody can do that, but on how could we motivate, encourage, and ignite a passion among our agents," recounted RE/MAX executive and longtime CMN Board member Mike Reagan. "As the agents embraced relationships a couple of wonderful things happened. They knew that one, the money would stay local to their hospital, and two, they realized that the kids and the families affected were the children of their clients, their own children, their co-workers' children. So it made it very personal from the very beginning, and that was really the foundation.

"One of my most fond memories," Reagan continued, "was February of 1992 at our RE/MAX convention in Atlanta. There were 4,500 RE/MAX folks there at the Fox Theatre and we introduced the Miracle Home program and from the beginning everyone just welcomed it and embraced it. Then two nights later at our awards show Marie Osmond and her son, Steve, who was about nine years old, performed for us. Everyone was so excited to realize someone of Marie's stature would come and be so friendly and open to everyone and let them know they were a part of something great."

Over the years, CMN would make no more valuable friend than Drayton McLane of Temple, Texas. Drayton was on the Board of Trustees at Scott & White Medical Center in Temple and was CEO of the McLane Company, the largest wholesaler distributing company in the country. Among McLane's customers were some 30,000 convenience stores, including big chains like 7-Eleven, Circle K, Wawa, Stop-N-Go, and Speedway. The chief development officer at Scott & White introduced us to Drayton, recognizing the possibilities of a relationship between the convenience store operators and Children's Miracle Network.

From our first meeting, Drayton, a deeply religious and ethical man who taught Sunday School at the First Baptist Church, brought his bigger-than-life personality to the cause. He did nothing halfway or at half speed. There's the story of the day he reached into his pocket, pulled out his checkbook, and wrote a check for $114 million to buy the Houston Astros baseball team. This was a man who had $114 million in his checking account!

Over the course of three years, Drayton's influence resulted in nine different convenience store chains signing on to partner with Children's Miracle Network, representing thousands of stores. This suited Eleanor's paper balloon icon program fundraiser perfectly. These 1000s of stores wound up raising hundreds of millions of dollars.

Workplace Fundraising struck cords with corporations large and small. Ace Hardware started a very popular bicycle tour from Chicago to Denver; its individual stores sold candy bars and Miracle Balloons. The Rite Aid drugstore chain enlisted great support from its hundreds of stores, coming up with the idea of putting money-saving coupons on the balloons. An associate at the Rite Aid store in Eugene, Oregon, named Wilson Paul "Buddy" Hazelton, was legendary in his support for Children's Miracle Network. When he was three years old, Buddy was hit by a car and dragged seventy-five feet. It was feared he would never walk again, if he survived at all. But he was rushed to a children's hospital and after five days in a coma, he gained consciousness and not only survived, but learned to walk in site of his left arm and hand being partially paralyzed.

Buddy's loyalty to children's hospitals came out loud and clear every year during the Miracle Balloon campaign at Rite Aid Store #5375 in Eugene. For more than twenty years, until his retirement, his enthusiastic salesmanship helped the store raise at least $5,000 each year for Eugene's Peace Health Sacred Heart Medical Center.

Buddy Hazelton is legendary for his twenty-year support of Children's hospitals

Another early sponsor was the Utah Credit Union League. The program they developed was ideal to be embraced by credit union leagues across the country. In the tradition of going-for-it, the Texas and California leagues were sought and secured first, leading the way for the rest of the nation. By the 2000's, over 5,000 credit unions nationwide were participating in fundraisers under the umbrella "Credit Unions for Kids."

Food Lion, a chain of 1,100 grocery stores in the south, was another early corporate sponsor, brought on thanks to Brett Hutchens. The Food Lion CEO, Tom Smith, became a member of the CMN Board of Governors.

In 1990, Max Burdick, one of our more energetic and successful salespeople, brought in the International Order of Foresters Life Insurance Company, an organization that would be worth its weight in gold in supporting the radiothon campaign (more on that in a later chapter). Burdick also brought in a group of truckers in North Carolina who hauled logs for a living. I thought he was kidding when he told me about them. "Go get a real sponsor," I said. But he wasn't kidding. The log-haulers joined with others in the logging industry to form a yearly fundraising program they called Log A Load For Kids, whereby truckers would donate a portion of the proceeds from their loads to CMN's hospitals.

Julia Stewart, the CEO of IHOP, came up with the idea of donating a portion of sales on National Pancake Day to CMN. In a single day they raised $800,000.

Many companies contributed. Costco...Giant Food Stores... Publix Super Markets...Goody's Family Clothing...TD Bank... Speedway...RiteAid...Ace Hardware...Love's Travel Stops... IHOP...Log-a-Load...Panda...Delta Airlines...Marriott Vacation Clubs...Walt Disney...every year the list continued to grow.

From the very beginning, we both committed to each other. Our sponsors deserved exclusivity. In exchange for their support of CMN, they needed and deserved our support in return. If RE/MAX was our real estate partner, for example, we wouldn't work with other real estate companies. Our relationship with Dairy Queen meant not working with McDonald's or Burger King, and so on. These were gentleman agreements, nothing was written down, but everyone understood it was the right thing to do and a good way of doing business.

There was one exception, however, and it turned out to be a big one. Just a couple of years after we'd started working with Walmart and Sam's Club, I got a call from Dr. Ben Carson, the esteemed neurosurgeon (and 2016 presidential candidate) at Johns Hopkins Hospital in Maryland. Dr. Carson was well aware of Children's Miracle Network, as we featured one of his patients in a Miracle Child story. Dr. Carson was on the Board of Costco, the big wholesale warehouse company headquartered outside Seattle in Issaquah, Washington. He suggested that CMN and Costco would be a good fit. Johns Hopkins was one of our valued hospital partners so as a courtesy I accepted Dr. Carson's invitation to travel with him to Washington for a meeting with Jim Sinegal, the co-founder and CEO of Costco. Dr. Carson and I sat down with Jim and Bill Gates, Sr., who was also on the Costco Board.

I reported on the meeting with Costco a few weeks later at our CMN Board meeting, where Don Soderquist, the Walmart COO, was in attendance. "Costco is interested in us," I said. "But that's a non-starter because of our exclusivity agreement with Sam's Club," the Walmart-run wholesale warehouse business that was Costco's biggest competitor.

Don Soderquist spoke up instantly. "No," he said, "We're not going to do that. If Costco wants to support the hospitals and they want to help kids we can't keep them out." (**YOU GOTTA BE KIDDING!**)

Through the years, Walmart and Costco would comprise the biggest one-two fundraising punch in Children's Miracle Network history.

Brittany Rogers

Bestselling author Andy Andrews has been a big supporter of Children's Miracle Network through the years. Among the dozens of books he has written is *Miracles One at a Time*, a collection of stories about children who have been helped at CMN hospitals. For his book, Andy solicited letters from kids all across America, asking them to talk about their experiences as they dealt with their sicknesses or injuries.

Among the dozens who responded was little Brittany Rogers, a cute six-year-old blonde-haired girl from Tennessee. A year earlier, Brittany was standing in the yard when her father was cutting the grass. Unaware Brittany was there, he ran over her right leg and foot. Very quickly, a life-flight helicopter arrived and transported the young girl to **East Tennessee Children's Hospital** in Knoxville, where she was rushed into surgery. The toes on her foot couldn't be saved, but doctors were eventually able to fashion a new foot for her. Brittany became that year's Champion Kid from Tennessee and visited the White House and attended the 1996 telethon festivities in Orlando.

Here, verbatim, is what Brittany wrote in her own hand about her experiences:

Hi Andy,

My name is Brittany Rogers and I am 6 ½ years old. I am home-schooled and in the first grade. I like pizza, ice cream, and going to church. I also like going to gymnastics, playing with my little sister, Holly, and my puppy, Brandie.

On May 23, 1995, I was outside playing. Daddy was mowing the yard and found a baby bunny's nest. I thought they were neat. I asked Mommy if I could see them again and she said it was OK, but I didn't go see them. I remembered I needed to tell my Daddy something. He was on a riding mower and didn't know I was there. He backed up and ran over my right leg and foot.

They couldn't take care of me at the hospital close to home so I got to ride in a helicopter to Knoxville, TN, to East TN Children's Hospital. I had a lot of trips to the "Big White Room" or surgery. They took muscle from my back and made me a new foot, since my toes went to Heaven. The rest of my leg was hurt pretty bad. It doesn't hurt too much now. Mommy and Daddy say I can tell the weather better than they do on TV.

I had a bunch of doctors and nurses who took care of me, Dr. Smith, Dr. Madigan, Dr. Patterson, Dr. Queen, and Dr. Kellett. My favorite nurse was Mrs. Donna. She always came to take me to the Big White Room. I get to wear several different colored casts. One purple and then pink. Those are my favorite colors. I really love all the people that took care of me. They made me feel special. I liked having water gun fights with my nurses, those shots make great water guns. I still like to go visit my doctors and nurses.

During the 1996 CMN telethon I got to go to Washington and meet the President and Mrs. Clinton. I also got to meet Steve Young, Mary Lou Retton and Marie Osmond and John Schneider. They were all very nice to me. I also got to go to Disney World. That was really a fun weekend! I made many new friends during that time. I'll remember them in my prayers. I hope I can see them again.

If I had some advice I could give someone it would be: always stay away from big things you could get hurt on.

I want to thank you and CMN for working so hard to help kids like me. Because of all the money made, the hospital had equipment to help all the sick and hurt kids. Don't worry about me, because God and Dr. Smith made me better. Remember Jesus loves you and I do too.

Hugs and kisses,

Brittany Rogers

The essence of why Children's Miracle Network exists, from the eloquence of a six-year-old!

As a post script about Andy's book, I was asked to add my own story about CMN. I still get choked up when I remember the experience I shared and the emotion behind it. Here is a reprint:

Andy Andrews
P.O. Box 3709
Gulf Shores, AL 36547

Dear Andy:

I am blessed with countless memories of very special kids, their families
and the quiet courage they exhibited. Thanks to 170 children's hospitals, the
350,000 people who work there and literally millions who support their efforts,
most of these kids go on to lead normal healthy lives.

Obviously, not all do. Tragically not all can be saved.

I met a couple whose fourth child was being treated in a newborn intensive
care unit. The baby had never left the hospital having received the most intense
and sophisticated care available for all four months of its life. Complications too
numerous to detail afflicted this baby. Despite the heroic efforts of the doctor
and nurses the baby had no chance of survival.

The parents were in a corner of the Newborn Intensive Care Unit agonizing
over the decision to let go. Upon hearing Marie and I were touring the unit
they interrupted their very private moment and asked me to come over. They
were aware Marie and I were members of their faith. They explained that after
four months it was time to let their precious baby go in peace.

They hugged me and thanked me for Children's Miracle Network and all it does.
They shared how grateful they were for caring, compassionate doctors and
nurses who had fought to save their baby. They asked me to thank Marie and
the Osmonds for all they do for children's hospitals and children in need. They
encouraged me to keep up this work to support this very special place that had
dominated the last four months of their lives.

We shared some tears, some hugs and prayed together. It was a prayer of
thanks for that special baby, that special hospital, and those special care-givers.

I am thankful for whatever we at Children's Miracle Network can do to ease the
pain of children and families whenever and wherever possible.

Thanks Andy.

Sincerely,

Mick Shannon
Co-Founder
President and CEO

Joe with Jack Lindquist, president of Disneyland, and Mick

....

CHAPTER TWENTY-TWO

Match Made in Heaven

After holding our first four CMN telethons at the incomparable Osmond Studios, it became clear we needed to find another location for our broadcast. For a very basic reason: the Osmonds had sold the studios.

All the members of the Osmond family made it clear they would continue to support Children's Miracle Network in every way they possibly could. No one doubted that. It is hard to imagine a family of celebrities doing any more for a charitable cause. It is not a stretch to say that without having their name and endorsement in the early going CMN would not have survived. It would be easier to list what the Osmonds DIDN'T do. They put on benefit concerts so we could pay our bills and cover our operating expenses in the front office. It was their name that got us our first major telethon production sponsor, Duff's Smorgasbord, without which we might have never made it to year two. Marie and Donny each played big roles in helping land Walmart. Bob Hope was just the beginning of the long list of celebrities who joined the effort directly because of the Osmonds. Marie took her role as co-founder very seriously, visiting children's hospitals and filming Children's Miracle Network spots wherever her performing schedule took her. She and her brother Jimmy served on our Board of Trustees.

Through all of this service, not a single Osmond asked for reimbursement or any other kind of payment. Ever.

One story illustrates the family's willingness to go wherever and do whatever was asked of them: In the critical early years, we were trying to land TV station WLS in Chicago. Chicago was a major market and we really needed a presence there. But WLS turned us down because they were already doing the cerebral palsy national telethon. The next time we were in town we called and asked the station manager, Dennis Swanson, if we could come by and talk some more. He said okay, although he insisted his position hadn't changed.

But we had the Osmonds.

The entire family was in Chicago for a concert. They agreed to go with us to see Dennis. When we got to the office building in downtown Chicago where WLS was located, we called up and asked Dennis if he'd come down to meet us in the lobby. When he got off the elevator, all seven Osmonds were there to greet him. Needless to say, we got the deal. As he turned to leave Dennis looked at Joe and me. "You guys don't play fair," he said.

So wherever we staged our fifth telethon, we knew we could count on the Osmonds performing, we just weren't going to do it in Orem.

To move on, our fondest hope was that we could form a relationship with Disney and Disneyland. From day one, that was our dream. What better place to associate a cause that was all about children than with the happiest place on earth? We would be able to utilize a variety of iconic backdrops and shots for the telecast. Every year since we incorporated, Joe had called Mike Davis, who was head of Disney's entertainment division, to talk about the prospects of a collaboration. Every year he had been told we weren't big enough. An understandable response as we found our footing and started to grow. But by year four, we had expanded to 130 hospitals from coast to coast.

If we couldn't get Disneyland, our thinking was that another large theme park would make a great setting for the telethon. To help us with our transition, Bill Critchfield, president of the Osmond Studios, had mentioned this to contacts he knew at Sea World in San Diego. In turn, Sea World contacted us and invited us to come to San Diego for a meeting to discuss the possibilities. Joe and I flew to San Diego and quickly discovered that the Sea World people had done their homework about the rapid growth and reach of our telethon. They absolutely wanted us to put on our next show at their park. They were ready to sign a contract then and there.

But as Joe and I drove from San Diego to the John Wayne Airport in Orange County mulling over the Sea World offer, we both had the same thought: *if we take Sea World we'll never get Disney.*

Before we did anything, we felt we had to give Disney one more try.

The next day, Joe called Mike Davis. Again.

"What is it going to take to get a meeting with Disney?" he pleaded.

Tongue in cheek, Davis said, "You're going to have to talk to Michael Eisner."

There was no more prominent executive in America at that time than Michael Eisner, Disney's CEO. He ran the Disney empire that covered two coasts and multiple businesses. Getting through to him would be like getting into the Kremlin.

"Well, give me his number then," said Joe.

Mike gave Joe the number for the Disney executive offices in Burbank.

Having nothing to lose, Joe—sitting in our tiny office in Salt Lake City—picked up the phone and called the number.

The person who answered the phone in Mr. Eisner's office asked who was calling.

"Joe Lake, from the Osmond Foundation's Children's Miracle Network Telethon."

Joe decided it couldn't hurt dropping the Osmond name.

Eisner, it turned out, had a history with the Osmonds. Years before he became president and Chairman of the Board of Walt Disney Company, he had been a production assistant on the *Donny & Marie Show*. He did not personally meet Donny and Marie or the rest of the family, but his experience was a positive one. Hearing "Osmond" piqued his interest.

Joe heard a voice come on the line.

"This is Michael Eisner, how can I help you?"

Joe was only hoping to make an appointment with an underling for a meeting, or even to make an appointment to make an appointment for a meeting. Now he had the floor to make his sales pitch over the phone.

As succinctly as he could, Joe laid out what we were doing and why we wanted to do it with Disney. To his surprise, Eisner stayed on the line and asked a number of follow-up questions, which Joe did his best to answer.

After a pause, Eisner said, "I think this is a good idea. But you're going to have to talk to Jack Lindquist. He's the president of Disneyland. Everything about the park goes through him. He'd have to make the decision."

"Great, I'll call Jack," said Joe.

"Hold on," said Eisner. "I'll call Jack. Give me twenty-four hours. Then I'll have him call you."

Click.

Cradling the phone, Joe didn't quite know how to react. In a phone call that lasted less than five minutes he had gotten an "I think this is a good idea" from Michael Eisner himself.

He came into my office.

"You're not going to believe what just happened," he said.

I said, "Holy crap!"

Any fears that Jack Lindquist wouldn't call quickly disappeared when Joe's phone rang the next day. It was Lindquist. He asked if we could fly to Anaheim for a discussion.

We met at a restaurant called Mr. Stox just down the street from Disneyland. You could see the Matterhorn from where we were dining.

If you wanted to pick somebody to represent Disney you'd pick Jack Lindquist, as lovable and engaging a man as you'd ever want to meet. His history with Disney went all the way back to the days when Walt Disney was walking the Anaheim strawberry field before it became Disneyland. He was one of the park's very first employees. He'd seen it all. Jack always had a big smile on his face. He had one on when he met us at Mr. Stox. Every indication was that this was going to go well.

In his autobiography, *In Service to the Mouse, my unexpected journey to becoming Disneyland's first president,* Jack wrote this about what transpired:

One morning, in the early spring of 1987, I got a call from Michael Eisner's office asking me to meet with a couple of gentlemen, Joe Lake and Mick Shannon, who had contacted him regarding having a charity event that would originate at Disneyland...Michael told me to hear them out, but the decision was mine.

I met with Joe and Mick the next afternoon for lunch at Mr. Stox in Anaheim. They represented Marie Osmond and John Schneider. The four of them are the co-founders of The Children's Miracle Network...Joe and Mick were looking for a new venue that would give them more exposure in a market that would offer closer access to participating celebrities. Their primary corporate supporters at that time were Marriott Corporation, Dairy Queen, Re/Max Realty, and Ace Hardware.

Joe and Mick wanted Disneyland to become the new home of Children's Miracle Network.

Now, there are many times in a career when opportunity just falls into your lap, and that opportunity makes all the sense in the world. Children's hospitals, the Osmonds, appearances by Miracle kids, 21 hours of live television, and Disneyland— talk about a no-brainer!

I told Joe and Mick that we were in. Disneyland would provide Videopolis as the home base for the telethon. We would work with them to locate other possible Disneyland locations for pre-taping of segments or live segments that would be used on the show. We would not sell tickets beyond our normal advertised hours, but we would allow guests in the park to stay and watch the TV show as long as they liked.

I told Joe and Mick that they would be billed for any additional production and technical costs incurred by Disneyland for bringing their live show to the park. I estimated that it would not be more than $350,000. They were ecstatic. We agreed to meet with our teams at the Anaheim Marriott Hotel within the next two weeks. Our team, which was headed by Mike Davis of our Entertainment Division, met with the CMN team and everything moved forward splendidly and speedily.

(YOU GOTTA BE KIDDING!)

Jack was right. We were ecstatic. It's true, we were facing a $350,000 fee for production costs, which was $350,000 more than we had ever paid, not to mention $350,000 that we didn't have. But all were in agreement that it was a move that made sense regardless and at our next Board meeting we included a $350,000 deficit in the budget. It was something we'd never done before and would never do again. But this was Disney, so we did it. Preparations for the upcoming telethon began immediately. From the outset, the Disney people couldn't have been more accommodating, and the same went for the management and staff at the Anaheim Marriott. The Marriott Corporation turned the enormous convention hotel over to us to use as our telethon headquarters and committed to providing rooms free of charge for all our celebrities and their families during the weekend of the show. Just a couple of months remained before the telethon. I marveled at how quickly everything started coming together.

As part of our planning, we needed to find a venue suitable for our sponsor's luncheon. In Utah, our tradition was to hold a reception at Alan Osmond's backyard on Saturday before the telethon began. The party gave us a chance to acknowledge everyone's contribution and thank them for their support.

We wanted to continue doing the lunch at Disneyland. After some searching, Jack said, "I can't give you a backyard, but I can donate Club 33."

He'd offered us the most exclusive, hard-to-get-into place in all of Disneyland.

Club 33 is located in New Orleans Square, above the Pirates of the Caribbean ride. Its name pays tribute to the thirty-three original investors who helped Walt Disney finance his dream park. Through the years it had gained a mythical stature—an intimate, private, by-invitation-only club in the heart of the Magic Kingdom. It held about thirty people. Just enough for us to invite our biggest sponsors, among them Joe Viviano from Hershey, Don Shinkle from Walmart, Todd Clist from Marriott, Bill Egan from Johnson & Johnson, Gary See from Dairy Queen, and Vinny Tracy from RE/MAX.

Michael Eisner, Jack Lindquist, and Frank Wells welcomed everyone on behalf of Disney. Our telethon hosts, Merlin Olsen, Marilyn McCoo, Mary Hart, Marie Osmond, and John Schneider, welcomed everyone on behalf of Children's Miracle Network. When they handed the microphone to me to make a few remarks I looked down at Michael Eisner and asked him what had caused him to take Joe's phone call. That's when we learned about his connection with the Osmonds.

Eisner looked over at Marie. "You're not going to remember this," he said, "But I was an assistant director on your show. When I heard this had something to do with the Osmonds, I was curious, so I took the call."

Michael Eisner could not have been more welcoming or engaging. During a casual lunch conversation, he mentioned an amazing news story that had just taken place. A young German teenager had landed his small plane in Red Square in Moscow, completely undetected by Russian security. "I'm going to make a movie about this," he told us. "Disney is first and foremost a movie studio."

When Merlin Olsen stood up to make his remarks, it started to rain outside and he saw a mouse—an actual mouse—run across the room. He remarked about Mickey Mouse personally coming to greet us and everyone laughed. It was a most auspicious start to what would prove to be a wonderful relationship.

Disney and Disneyland were magical for Children's Miracle Network, and vice versa. We provided basically a twenty-one-hour commercial for Disney. They provided the perfect setting for us. The main stage was at Videopolis, the almost brand new (it opened in 1985) 5,000-square-foot amphitheatre located in Fantasyland. But when we suggested taping segments at other locations, showing off all that Disneyland had to offer, everyone was more than agreeable. We shot Marie riding in a float down Main Street with Disney characters while singing a Disney song. We shot Mary Hart performing a Snow White number with the prince on a white horse. We brought our seasoned telethon production crew, headed by Al Henderson (Mike Mischler had by now moved his talents to CBS), and they meshed seamlessly with the Disney people. (Disney ended up hiring Al and the Video West crew to produce their Christmas parade. The Disney people said it was the best crew they had ever worked with.)

And while the Osmond Studios had been a big draw, Disneyland was even bigger. Hardly anyone in the entertainment business turned Joe down when he called. For years, he made it a goal to book the group with the number one song on Billboard the month of the telethon, and more often than not he was successful. We had Fleetwood Mac one year, Tony Orlando & Dawn the next. Sammy Davis, Jr., Dean Martin, Wayne Newton, the Commodores, Sister Sledge, Robert Goulet (who, while performing *The Impossible Dream*, forgot the words), Rich Little, Kenny Loggins. They all performed, at the height of their game, and that's just for starters.

Running a twenty-one hour live telethon gets you up close and personal with the entertainers. Sometimes a little too up close and personal. During one show, a band was rehearsing behind the curtain and making a lot of noise on the stage while we were live on the air. I stormed back stage to tell them to knock it off. The first person I ran into was Mick Fleetwood of Fleetwood Mac. Now Mick Fleetwood is 6-foot-7. I looked up and stopped immediately, and said, in a kind, gentle voice, "Hey guys, I was wondering if maybe you could hold it down a little?"

Filling the early morning hours on Sunday, when no one's watching but night watchmen and insomniacs, was always interesting. One year we turned the hosting duties at three o'clock in the morning over to Jim Harbaugh, the football coach who later on would take the San Francisco 49ers to the Super Bowl. At the time, Harbaugh was playing quarterback in the NFL for the Indianapolis Colts. We asked him and fellow NFL quarterback Warren Moon to host the early morning segments while sitting on the stairs in front of the Disney Castle, and ad lib in between the acts with some CMN pep talks, which we thought would be a natural for a quarterback. For some reason, Warren went to take a potty break, leaving Harbaugh sitting on the steps all by himself—with America out there watching. He became tongue-tied. He couldn't think of anything to say. "Warren, get over here! Where the hell are you! I need you!" Harbaugh shouted into a live mic. I don't know how many people were watching at three in the morning, but of course we'd captured the whole thing on tape, and later gave it to the football staff at Stanford, where Harbaugh had become head coach. They played it in a film practice session so they could tease the coach. Watching it all those years later, Harbaugh laughed harder than anybody.

For our CMN family of sponsors, hospitals, miracle children, staff, and celebrities, Disneyland became *the* place; our home away from home the last weekend of May. Disney gave us 3,000 tickets to the park so everyone could take their guests to Disneyland. It was amazing what a draw that was. No matter how famous someone was or how much money they made, getting to bring the family to Disneyland was appealing. A fun perk. On a number of occasions Disney closed the park to the public at night and kept it open for our private party.

For that first Disneyland telethon in 1987, Michael Eisner, after hosting everyone at lunch at Club 33, agreed to tape a segment for us before he left for home. In the clip, he greeted everyone to the telethon and welcomed them to Disneyland. He then said, "This is possibly the best thing we've ever done at Disneyland." When the show went on the air at nine o'clock Saturday night, that was our opening. All the money in the world can't pay for that kind of sincere endorsement. We were off and running.

Twenty-one hours later, at six o'clock Sunday evening, Marie, John, Marilyn, Merlin, and Mary were joined on stage with the Miracle Children, assorted Disney characters, and Disneyland president Jack Lindquist. Thanks to Walmart's $2.1 million check, other sponsor checks, and a record number of callers, the tote board showed more than $41 million, a twenty-five percent increase from the previous year. And that wasn't all. Jack Lindquist had one more bit of Disney magic up his sleeve.

Here's how he recounted it in his book, *In Service to the Mouse*:

"I watched the show from home the rest of the day and returned to the park at around two in the afternoon. I was scheduled to do a bit with Marie at 3:15 and then participate in the close with Marie and John, as well as Mickey, Minnie, Pluto, Goofy, and Donald. Marie repeatedly thanked me for having Children's Miracle Network at Disneyland. She said

that she hoped it would go on forever. Then, she grabbed my cheeks and said to the audience, "He's just so darn cute! I want to hug him." Then, she gave me a big hug and kiss. I love show biz!

During the closing, I slipped an envelope into John Schneider's pocket. We were on the air, and Joe and Mick had already instituted a policy not to open any sealed envelopes on the air in case they contained inappropriate messages or anything like that. Following the segment, John took the unopened envelope to Joe and Mick at the producer's table. Joe and Mick were standing together when they unsealed the envelope and found their Disney bill ripped into pieces. (YOU GOTTA BE KIDDING!)

That year, CMN raised more than $41 million for children's hospitals throughout North America. Moving the event to Disneyland raised $10 million more than the previous year

Children's Miracle Network's association with Disneyland and Walt Disney World proved to be the Mouse that laid a golden egg. It's nice to be part of a no-brainer, now and then."

We stayed at Disneyland seven years before relocating, at Disney's request, to Disney World in Orlando, Florida, where the relationship continued to flourish. Those seven years we were in California, Jack Lindquist and his Disneyland family never wavered in treating us like royalty, and never charged us a single penny for our production costs.

LESLIE HANCOCK

Six-year-old Leslie Hancock of Dubuque, Iowa, needed help and she needed it fast.

Leslie had been born with cystic fibrosis, or CF, a hereditary disease that affects the cells that produce mucus, sweat, and digestive juices, resulting in thickened mucus that blocks the lungs, pancreas, and other organs, impeding their proper usage.

After surgery to remove a blockage of her intestine right after she was born, Leslie's first years living with CF were relatively healthy. But when she was five she started to tire easily and her abdomen began to swell—telltale signs of liver disease. Tests confirmed that Leslie had severe cirrhosis of the liver due to her CF. Without a liver transplant she would be dead in months.

Michelle Kwan and Leslie Hancock

She had two options. The first was to place her name at the end of the long line of people waiting for a liver from an organ donor. The second was to receive a liver from a close relative—a living donor.

Leslie's parents, Wendy and Jim Hancock, did not hesitate when they learned of the second option. They had no time to waste. Jim was immediately tested. He turned out to be a perfect match. Six weeks after turning six, Leslie became the first child in Iowa history to undergo a living donor liver transplant.

The procedure took place at the **University of Iowa Hospitals & Clinics**, a CMN-affiliated institution. On the morning of the surgery, Wendy Hancock sent both her husband and daughter into surgery. She then went to the waiting room to endure a nerve-wracking fourteen-hour wait no mother and wife should ever have to endure.

Fifteen medical specialists, led by liver transplant surgeons Maureen Martin, M.D., and Youmin Wu, M.D., performed the historic procedure. After a very long and tense day, as soon as they could see that Leslie's new liver was functioning properly, the operating room erupted into cheers.

Leslie was able to return home and resume a happy childhood. Months later, she appeared as a CMN Champion during the annual Children's Miracle Network broadcast at Disney World. A highlight of her weekend was meeting and talking with Olympic skating medalist—and ardent CMN supporter—Michelle Kwan, who praised her effusively for her bravery and strength.

Bo Jackson with Jason Wright

....

CHAPTER TWENTY-THREE

World Leaders and Celebrities

From day one, the generosity of celebrities was the engine that drove the Children's Miracle Network.

The parade of selfless influencers began with co-founders John Schneider and Marie Osmond and never stopped. The support came from anywhere and everywhere. A case in point is the 1992 telethon, when we aired video packages of Pope John Paul II, Princess Diana, and President George H.W. Bush—each of them visiting CMN hospitals. The Pope, the Princess, and the President.

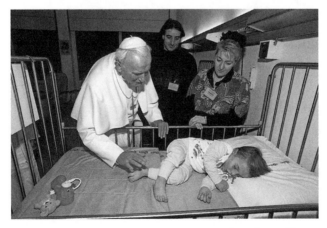

Pope John Paul II visits children at the Izaak Walton Killam Children's Hospital in Halifax, Nova Scotia.

Pope John Paul II had visited children at the Izaak Walton Killam Children's Hospital in Halifax, Nova Scotia, a CMN member hospital. The people at Izaak Killam obtained permission from the Vatican to film the Pope's visit and the Canadian Broadcasting System agreed to shoot the piece for us. The Papal plane was at the airport and the city had come to a virtual standstill. Huge crowds followed the Pope wherever he went. Media was everywhere. Only a handful of people were allowed in the hospital to accompany the Pope as he visited the children. The Pope went from room to room, talking with the kids and blessing them. Being in the presence of the Pope was overwhelming, a profoundly spiritual and moving experience.

Princess Diana and Prince Charles visit the Jane Way Children's Hospital in St. John's, Newfoundland.

On their countrywide tour of Canada in June of 1983, Princess Diana and Prince Charles had visited the Jane Way Children's Hospital in St. John's, Newfoundland. The Jane Way staff managed to produce a very powerful and emotional video of Princess Diana visiting with the children. She treated the children with such gentleness, making eye contact with them and touching them. She didn't seem to care who was in the room or who was watching. She paid no attention to the cameras, she was totally focused on the kids. She had an aura of kindness about her.

U.S. presidents through the years have frequently visited the kids at Children's National Hospital in Washington, D.C. President Bush—the first one—agreed to visit the kids there. He was in his last year in the White House. I did not fly to Washington for the filming, leaving the production in the hands of the local television station that carried our CMN telethon. They did a terrific job, and it was the beginning of a long relationship with CMN and the U.S. Presidency. In years to come, Presidents Clinton, the second Bush, and Obama would also all actively and enthusiastically support CMN while they were in the White House.

Through the years, literally thousands of celebrities and public figures, from entertainers, to sports stars, to politicians, to everything and everyone in between, have given freely of their time and talents to CMN. We paid just one appearance fee over the years, just one, and that was to the hottest celebrity in the country at the time—$100,000 to Bill Cosby, plus $20,000 for his private jet. We have since felt that was a mistake and have regretted it ever since. The simple truth was, celebrities and famous people were ready and willing to give back for no compensation. Helping and caring for sick children was enough. It brought out the best in a lot of very nice people— and raised a tremendous amount of money and awareness for the cause.

Initially, our celebrities were entertainers, beginning with our co-founders John Schneider and Marie Osmond, and continuing with Marilyn McCoo, Billy Davis Jr., Mary Hart, Bob Hope, et al. Merlin Olsen was an entertainer *and* an athlete. Over time, sports stars, such as Steve Young and Mary Lou Retton, would join the lineup.

The telethon was a natural attraction for entertainers to utilize their talents on a big stage to a national audience, while also displaying their compassionate and caring side. We had some of the biggest acts in show business, but also gave opportunities to up-and-comers. Jeff Foxworthy made his very first national TV appearance on our telethon. So did actor Kevin Pollak, and the American Dream Juggling Team. (Joe "discovered" them all.) Celine Dion did a remote from Canada, marking her first time on American TV. We were responsible for starting the romance between actress Cathy Lee Crosby and football star Joe Theismann when they met on one of our shows.

But the telethon was just the start of it. Many celebrities from a variety of arenas contributed their name and fame in a variety of ways and formats throughout the year. And it didn't seem to matter how busy they were; somehow they'd find time for CMN.

Bo Jackson, for example. In the late 1980s, Bo was the most famous athlete in the world, an all-star in the National Football League *and* Major League Baseball. Before that, he'd won the Heisman Trophy as the nation's top college football player, besides starring on the baseball team at Auburn University and running on the track team. He may be the greatest athlete who ever lived. Todd Christensen, a loyal CMN supporter since his playing days at BYU, was a teammate of Bo's in the NFL when both played for the Los Angeles Raiders. Todd knew Bo had a big heart and loved kids, and felt he would be a good fit for CMN. He set up a meeting for me to meet with Bo at the Marina del Ray Marriott, where Bo was living while playing with the Raiders. He told Bo the CEO of Children's Miracle Network was coming to meet him. But as the meeting got closer, I couldn't make it. I had committed to coach my son Matthew's Junior Jazz basketball team. The coach couldn't miss the first game. It was against all the values I had taught the players over the first two weeks of practice. You know, responsibility, teamwork, always being on time. Stuff like that. Missing the first game would have made me a hypocrite.

Fortunately, Joe agreed to go in my place. Still, I felt I owed Bo an explanation as to why the CEO wasn't able to be there in person. I explained in a letter, "The coach simply can't let his kids down in the first game of the season." (We all know Joe is much better at this than I am anyway.)

Joe entered Bo's room and sat on the bed while Bo read the letter. Bo looked up and said, "I'm in." And was he ever. Nike had built a major advertising campaign around Bo called "Bo Knows." We did "Bo Knows Kids." Bo came to Salt Lake to cut a spot with kids as if visiting a children's hospital. In it, he finishes a grueling working as the narrator says, "Bo Jackson pedals and pumps his way through a demanding workout routine almost every day, but Bo's biggest lift comes long after his workout day is over." The next scene is Bo visiting a child at his hospital bedside. The child's face lights up when he sees Bo, as the narrator continues, "Knowing that nearly five million children in hospitals all over the country are being helped through the Children's Miracle Network is enough to give anyone a lift."

Bo paid visits to Miracle Network hospitals from one end of the country to the other. Everything we asked of him, he willingly did. Even after he broke his hip and his amazing two-sport career ended, Bo Jackson never stopped being all-in for kids.

Sports stars could attract attention and publicity by what they did on the playing field, and off. Jim McMahon was a great example of that. Jim had been with us ever since he accompanied John Schneider on the March of Dimes Walkathon before anyone knew who he was. Less than a decade later, in 1985, he was the quarterback of what has been called the greatest professional football team ever—the Super Bowl champion Chicago Bears. McMahon was the undisputed, if irreverent, leader of that Bears team. Everything he did got noticed. During a playoff game he wore a headband with the name of one of his sponsors, ADIDAS. Pete Rozelle, the commissioner of the NFL, fined McMahon $5,000 for violating league policy that prohibited the advertising of products during a game. McMahon answered back by wearing a headband that spelled out ROZELLE at the next game. Rozelle said he was amused but the $5,000 fine still stood. The headband controversy became a big story.

Then the Bears moved on to the Super Bowl...and we saw an opportunity.

I thought to myself, *this is too good to be true. I've got to get some headbands to Jim.*

Merlin Olsen was working on the broadcast of Super Bowl XX in New Orleans. We made up some headbands with SUPPORT CHILDREN'S HOSPITALS labeled on the front and shipped them to Merlin, who got them to McMahon. Sure enough, during pregame warmups, there was McMahon, wearing our headband in full view of a nationwide television audience of 93 million people. The next day, a picture of McMahon and the headband taken by an Associated Press photographer was on the front page of newspaper sports sections throughout the country.

Steve Young was another superstar quarterback who was involved with us from the very beginning. After Steve turned pro, he introduced us to his agent, Leigh Steinberg, who was also a very charity-minded individual. Leigh created the Quarterback Club for NFL quarterbacks to help them build a branding niche and offer their likenesses to advertisers. About a dozen members of the club were his own clients, who he helped set up their own charitable foundations. On one memorable afternoon during the Pro Bowl week in Hawaii, members of the Quarterback Club agreed to take time out of their schedules to get together and shoot a spot for Children's Miracle Network. The group—half of whom would make the Hall of Fame—included John Elway, Jim Kelly, Jim Harbaugh, Drew Bledsoe, Warren Moon, Boomer Esiason, Dan Marino, Randall Cunningham, Phil Simms, Bernie Kosar, Troy Aikman, and Steve Young. The spot called for the quarterbacks to talk about their favorite plays. It ends with the narrator saying, "The best play is helping children; it's working wonders."

Leigh Steinberg definitely caught the vision of CMN, always going out of his way to make sure his clients were available whenever possible. In 1996, when he was the most famous sports agent in the business (the hit movie released that year with Tom Cruise, *Jerry Maguire*, was based on Leigh), he decided to have some fun with our Board of Trustees. Under the letterhead of STEINBERG & MOORAD, he wrote this letter, tongue firmly in cheek, to John Vice, president of the CMN Board of Trustees:

June 24, 1996

Dear Mr. Vice,

Congratulations to you and all the members of the CMN Board for an outstanding 14th Annual CMN Broadcast. My clients, Steve Young, Warren Moon, Drew Bledsoe and others, all had a great time and we are proud of our association with a quality organization such as CMN.

Mick Shannon, President/CEO, and Joseph Lake, Executive Vice President, deserve a lot of credit for the past outstanding year. Additionally, they have indicated to me that you will be working on the CMN Executive Compensation Committee in reviewing their salary and benefits.

Please be advised that I have now added Lake and Shannon to my client base. Please direct all discussions regarding their upcoming contract negotiations towards my office. I will look forward to meeting with you in the near future to discuss the terms and conditions for the future compensation of Lake and Shannon. I am sure that when their stellar performance over the last year is factored into their years of dedication and outstanding service, a mutual satisfying agreement will be reached in the near future.

Both the clients and staff of Steinberg & Moorad look forward to many future years of affiliation with CMN and your worthy endeavors.

Kindest personal regards,

Leigh Steinberg

It was all a gag, of course. Joe and I never had an agent or lobbied for anyone to "show me the money." It was just a good friend having fun and reflecting the esteem he had for Children's Miracle Network.

Legendary golfers Arnold Palmer and Jack Nicklaus were already involved with children's hospitals when Children's Miracle Network began, Jack with the Children's Hospital of Columbus (now Nationwide Children's Hospital), and Arnold with the Community Children's Hospital in Orlando, Florida (in 1989 it became the Arnold Palmer Hospital for Children.). The hospitals partnered with Jack at his annual event on the PGA Tour, the Memorial Tournament, and with Arnold at his tournament, the Arnold Palmer Invitational at Bay Hill. Barbara Nicklaus, Jack's wife, later joined the Children's Miracle Network Board of Trustees.

Joe, Jack Nicklaus, Mick, and Arnold Palmer

We commissioned an original portrait of Jack Nicklaus, and another one with Arnold Palmer and Bob Hope, printing 1,000 limited edition lithographs of each. Nicklaus, Palmer and Hope autographed them all and we sent them to hospitals all over the country to auction off as fundraisers. The items soon became collectibles, increasing in value with every year. The same thing happened with signed jerseys we got from the Dream Team, the fabled 1992 U.S. Olympic basketball team that won gold at the Barcelona Olympics. Indianapolis got Larry Bird's jersey, Los Angeles got Magic Johnson's. Chicago got Michael Jordan's, New York got Patrick Ewing's, Alabama got Charles Barkley's, Duke got Christian Laettner's, Primary Children's in Salt Lake City got Karl Malone's and John Stockton's, and so forth. We went to the practice, got all the autographs, and distributed the jerseys to the various hospitals. There is no telling how much those signatures did to help sick children.

It would be impossible to adequately chronicle all the good done by the hundreds of celebrities, entertainers, actors, athletes, coaches, and statesmen who have supported Children's Miracle Network over the years. With apologies to any who might have been left out, this is a list of many who freely and selflessly gave of their time and talents over the first thirty-six years, whether by performing at a telethon or in any other capacity:

A

Kimberly Aiken
Troy Aikman
Danny Ainge
Alabama
Jamie Alcroft
Domenick Allen
American Dream Juggling Team
John Amos
John Amos
Andy Andrews
Paul Anka
Appolonia
Ashford & Simpson

Patti Austin
Frankie Avalon
Margaret Avery

B

Johnny B
Jeff Bagwell
Thurl Bailey
Gary Baker
Jason Bateman
Ned Beatty
James Best
Kurt Bestor
Big & Rich
Stephen Bishop
Clint Black

Drew Bledsoe
Tempest Bledsoe
Lisa Bonet
Debby Boone
Pat Boone
Twitch Boss
Bruce Boxleitner
Shawn Bradley
Wayne Brady
Brandy
Jim Brickman
Garth Brooks
T. Graham Brown
Kobe Bryant
Gary Burghoff

George Burns
George H. W. Bush
George W. Bush
Laura Bush
Dean Butler

C

Kurt Cameron
Candace Cameron
Stephen J. Cannell
Nick Cannon
Gretchen Carlson
Karen Carpenter
Richard Carpenter
Diahann Carroll
Charlie Daniels Band
Joseph Jacques Jean Chrétien
Todd Christensen
Wang Chung
Bill Clinton
Hillary Clinton
Club Nouveau
The Commodores
Harry Connick Jr.
David Copperfield
Leanza Cornett
Bill Cosby
Stephen R. Covey
David Crosby
Cathy Lee Crosby
Randall Cunningham

D

Dallas Cowboy Cheerleaders
Michael Damien
Mac Davis
Eric Davis
Danny Davis & The Nashville Brass
Billy Davis Jr.
Sammy Davis Jr.
Chico DeBarge
Diamond Rio
the Fifth Dimension
Erica Dimpel
Celine Dion
Deidra Downs
Mack Dryden
Jeff Dunham
Ericka Dunlap

E

LaVell Edwards
John Elway
Boomer Esiason
Gloria Estefan
Linda Eyre
Richard Eyre

F

Nannette Fabray
Brett Favre
Mick Fleetwood and the Zoo
Michael J. Fox
Jeff Foxworthy

Linda Fratianne
Heather French
Hayden Fry

G

Danny Gans
Andy Gibb
Debbie Gibson
Glass Tiger
Lou Gosset Jr.
Robert Goulet
Amy Grant
Lee Greenwood
Ken Griffey Jr.
Scott Grimes

H

Kirsten Haglund
Jim Harbaugh
Katie Harman
Erika Harold
Art Harriman
Franco Harris
Mary Hart
Lisa Hartman
David Hasselhoff
Hunter Hayes
Joel Higgins
Russell Hitchcock
Allison Holker
Tara Dawn Holland
Clint Holmes
Lou Holtz
Bob Hope
Billy Hufsey

Larry Hughes

J

Reggie Jackson
Bo Jackson
Ronnie Jayne
The Jets
Nicole Johnson
Jonas Brothers

K

Laura Kaeppeler
Jim Kelly
Jayne Kennedy
Larry King
George Kirby
Kool & the Gang
Lon Kruger
Mike Krzyzewski
Michelle Kwan

L

Lady Antebellum
Valerie Landsburg
Carol Lawrence
The Lettermen
Eric Lindros
Rich Little
Rebecca Lobo
Heather Locklear
Kenny Loggins
Jennifer Lopez

M

Mack and Jamie
Kenneth Mack

Rick Majerus
Howie Mandel
Louise Mandrell
Dan Marino
Dean Martin
The Mary Jane Girls
Johnny Mathis
Marilyn McCoo
Michael McDonald
Maureen McGovern
The McGuire Sisters
Jim McMahon
Kristy McNichol
Glenn Medeiros
Mary Ann Mobley
Warren Moon

N

Graham Nash
Lauren Nelson
Juice Newton
Wayne Newton
Olivia Newton-John
Jack Nicklaus
Barbara Nicklaus
Gifford Nielsen

O

Oak Ridge Boys
Barack Obama
Michelle Obama
Edward James
Olmos
Merlin Olsen
Tony Orlando

Tom Osborne
Marie Osmond
Donny Osmond
Merrill Osmond
Alan Osmond
Jay Osmond
Wayne Osmond
Jimmy Osmond
Michael Osmond
Doug Osmond
Nathan Osmond
David Osmond

P

Arnold Palmer
Ray Parker Jr.
Joe Paterno
Dan Patrick
Sandi Patty
Nia Peeples
Kevin Pollak

R

Lou Rawls
Gene Anthony Ray
Collin Raye
Ronald Reagan
Christopher Reeve
Mary Lou Retton
Lionel Richie
Kathy Rigby
Diamond Rio
Robin Roberts
John Robinson
Kenny Rogers

Jalen Rose
Nolan Ryan

S

Carolyn Suzanne Sapp
Teresa Scanlan
John Schneider
Ricky Schroder
Dan Seals
T.G. Sheppard
Richard Sherman
Robert Sherman
Katherine Shindle
Sonny Shroyer
Ricky Skaggs
Sister Sledge
Emmitt Smith
Shawntel Smith
Michael W. Smith
Solid Gold Dancers
Suzanne Sommers

Mark Spitz
Frank Stallone
Katie Stam
Lee Steinberg
Lindsay Sterling
Connie Stevens
Michael Strahan
Kerri Strug
Sunshade 'n Rain
Air Supply
Raven Symone

T

The Taylors
Grant Teaff
John Tesh
Mark Tewksbury
Joe Theismann
B.J. Thomas
Bob Toledo
Debbye Turner

V

Marjorie Judith Vincent

W

Dee Wallace
Malcolm-Jamal Warner
Michael Warren
Dottie West
Heather Whitestone
Colm Wilkinson
Beau Williams
Deniece Williams
Paul Williams
Roger Williams
Marc Wilson
Shanice Wilson
Tom Wopat
Tammy Wynette

Y

Steve Young

MIRACLE CHILD:

DAVID PIERSON

Resiliency. Year after year, the recurring theme at children's hospitals coast to coast is the amazing attitudes of the children being cared for. Their ability to face their challenges with courage, equanimity, and cheerfulness inspires everyone around them.

Such was the case with fourteen-year-old David Pierson of Covington, Louisiana. David was driving an ATV in his driveway on the Fourth of July when the machine flipped and he landed on his head, breaking his jaw and collarbone, dislocating his kneecap, knocking out several teeth, and suffering cuts all over his body. David was rushed first to Lakeview Regional Medical Center in Covington and then, after the severity of his injuries were diagnosed, transported forty miles away to **Children's Hospital New Orleans,** where he underwent a nine-hour surgery. Miraculously, he emerged with no brain damage or long-term physical disability.

David's effervescent personality was also intact. During his lengthy hospital stay, in spite of all his injuries, he never wavered in maintaining his positivity and good humor. Dr. Michael Moses, David's plastic surgeon and president of the medical staff at Children's Hospital New Orleans, said, "He showed a maturity to deal with the pain and keep his sense of humor far beyond his years. He is such a non-complaining, positive-thinking, polite, nice kid who cares about others more than himself. He works hard, he's responsible, he's forward-thinking and he's grateful for what he has."

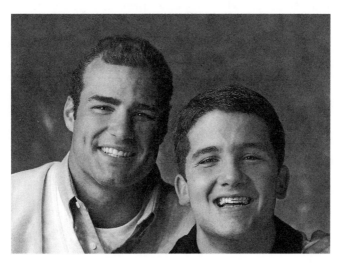

Philadelphia Flyers hockey star Eric Lindros with David Pierson

A year after the accident David returned to the hospital and underwent more surgery to reshape his nose and one of his eye sockets and finesse the scar on his lip.

His praise of the hospital and the attention he received was unequivocal. "The love and the care were just unbelievable," he said. "The nurses were my best friends. It was just constant joking with them. They always called me 'Popsicles' because that was the only thing I could eat. You could tell this wasn't just a job for them—they really cared.

"There are so many things we take for granted, like just walking down the street, being able to breathe on your own, having all your limbs. Staying positive, and being surrounded by positive people, really helped me. Doctors, nurses, my family and friends—they kept my spirits up."

At CMN Champions in Orlando, David was able to meet and have his picture taken with Philadelphia Flyers hockey star Eric Lindros. Eric started visiting kids in children's hospitals when he was a teenager in Toronto, a practice he continued after he become a professional hockey player and moved to Philadelphia. Meeting kids at CMN hospitals like David, he said, always gave him a lift. "At the end of the day I probably get more out of it than the kids do," he said.

Radiothon advertising for Riley Hospital for Children, Indianapolis

....

CHAPTER TWENTY-FOUR

Innovate and Grow Revenue

In a little over a decade Children's Miracle Network had found solid footing with 170 member hospitals, 200 television stations broadcasting the annual Memorial Day telethon (to more than 100 million households), and more than sixty corporate sponsors, all with ongoing Workplace Fundraising plans in place. We raised more money every year (by far) than Jerry Lewis's Labor Day telethon, or any other telethon in the world. We'd stayed true to "100 percent stays local" with no exceptions and ran the national organization with a staff of less than fifty full time employees, and no debt, thanks to separate underwriting contributions that paid the bills.

Our fundraising successes, coupled with positive reviews from nonprofit watchdog groups—organizations that monitored such things as office overhead and the percentage of funds raised actually making it to the intended recipients— brought us considerable attention from both companies and healthcare providers interested in forming a relationship with CMN. In 1990, I received a call from the development officer of the Mayo Clinic in Rochester, Minnesota, requesting a meeting. I agreed to fly to Minnesota and in advance ran all the numbers regarding our sponsor locations and telethon history to give the Mayo Clinic a good idea of what kind of money I thought they'd be able to raise every year as a telethon participant and recipient.

We sat down in the boardroom on the nineteenth floor of the Mayo Clinic's headquarters, an incredibly ornate and impressive place, reflecting the fact that this indeed was one of the world's most powerful, well-funded healthcare organizations on the planet.

I got right to the point. "I think you guys could probably do about $186,000 annually with the telethon," I said as I proceeded to produce the relevant facts and figures.

The development officer cleared his throat. "I can't go to lunch for $186,000," he said.

"I know that," I answered. "But you called me, I didn't call you."

That's when he said, "Well, let me tell you why we wanted to talk."

He informed me that the Mayo Clinic was interested in acquiring Children's Miracle Network. They were prepared to negotiate an appropriate price that would be several millions of dollars. By owning and running CMN, it would give them more in-house access and influence with our member hospitals, helping to further cement their reputation as the premiere healthcare provider in the country. It was a power play, pure and simple, and completely understandable on their part.

I took the proposal to the Board of Trustees, confident they would feel the same as me, that this was not going to be a practical option. We turned down the Mayo Clinic offer for the same reason we had turned down the NACHRI offer seven years earlier—because our first obligation and responsibility was to protect the integrity of our member hospitals and not sell or give away that control. As with the NACHRI offer, the Board said no thanks, but thanks very much for the compliment.

But flattery and books in the black never meant we intended to rest on our laurels. By 1995, after we'd moved the telethon to Walt Disney World in Florida, I had blueprints on the table for two new innovative programs that I felt had the potential of greatly increasing fundraising and awareness. We just had to figure out a way to pay for them.

At the Board meeting following the 1995 telethon, I laid out the two proposed programs for the trustees. One was called Champions Across America. The second was Radiothon.

In Champions, the idea was to designate one Miracle Child as a Champion in each of the fifty states in America and all twelve of the provinces in Canada. These sixty-two Champions, accompanied by their parents and siblings, would be flown either to the White House in Washington, D.C. or Parliament Hill in Ottawa, where they would meet with the president, the prime minister, or other heads of state. After that, they would continue their flight to Orlando for the CMN Telethon on Memorial Day Weekend. In addition to honoring the Champion kids, it was envisioned that the event would lend itself to media opportunities at every step along their journey. Air Canada and Delta Airlines had agreed to help transport the Champions and their families. Overall, I calculated the expenses for the annual program to be $400,000.

The idea to do a Radiothon came from Steve Rum, the development officer at Duke Children's Hospital. Steve suggested that we should talk to a radio executive named Bob Lind. Lind managed several radio stations in Raleigh, North Carolina, that together broadcast an annual fundraising marathon for Duke Children's Hospital that consistently brought in millions of dollars. Before coming to North Carolina, Bob had created and executed the same campaign for Johns Hopkins Hospital when he worked at a radio station in Baltimore. These radio fundraisers were essentially the same format as a telethon, without the visual of course. For anywhere from eighteen to twenty-two hours the station would devote all of its programming to raising money for the hospital, asking listeners to call in with pledges, while telling miracle child stories, promoting the local hospital and giving air time to participating sponsors. Bob Lind is considered the founder of Radiothon. Steve Rum felt it would be a perfect program for CMN and asked Bob to give me a call.

From the first conversation with Bob Lind I was sold, both on him and on Radiothon. He had been very successful in his career as a radio executive, but when I asked if he would be interested in coming to CMN and coordinating Radiothons throughout our network, he did not have to think about it before answering yes. He estimated he'd need a team of six to have things up and running. I calculated the expenses for Radiothon to be $600,000.

That meant that between Champions and Radiothon, I told the Board, we needed to find $1 million in order to be able to implement both programs.

When the Board meeting ended, Ken Peterson drifted over to talk to me privately. Ken was CEO of the International Order of Foresters, the financial services and life insurance company headquartered in Canada that had been a CMN sponsor since 1990. Much like the real estate agents at RE/MAX, Foresters agents located in cities and towns all around North America organized fundraisers to benefit their local children's hospitals. Foresters had a reputation as a company with a conscience. It began way back in 1874 as a fraternal organization in Canada, the International Order of Foresters. Its first philanthropic cause was building orphanages for children.

Ken asked if I'd come to Foresters' headquarters in Toronto and address all of their employees. A few weeks later I found myself in Toronto, addressing a room of about three hundred of their employees. I brought a Miracle Child with me, along with his parents, which was our usual M.O. when we spoke to groups. I introduced the young man, who had been treated successfully at The Hospital for SickKids in Toronto, along with his parents, and turned the microphone over to them to tell their story. When they were finished, I spent about fifteen minutes talking about where CMN had been, where we were today, and where we were going. As I finished up, Ken joined me on the stage. Ken was six-foot-six, a World War II veteran, and the kindest man you'll ever meet. He put his arm around me. "Before you leave," he said. "We want you to have this. We want you to proceed with Radiothon and Champions Across America and Canada." I looked down. He had just handed me a check for $1 million. I had a hard time holding back the tears. (**YOU GOTTA BE KIDDING!**)

Time and again I had seen this happen: good people stepping up, unbidden, to contribute what was needed to keep CMN moving forward. Gary Sheets. Brett Hutchens. Sam Walton. Jack Lindquist...Ken Peterson joined a long line of CMN benefactors, all motivated by no other reason than to help kids. I left Toronto convinced yet again that I had the greatest job in the world.

Bob Lind, the founder of Radiothon, came to work for us almost immediately. He turned in his notice to the radio station group in Raleigh and accepted our job offer, which paid him quite a bit less than what he had been making. Bob was nonplussed. Passion was his currency. I had never met anyone quite like Bob. He couldn't take yes for an answer. I would be on the phone with him and he'd ask for this and that and I'd say yes and yes. Then he'd say, "I also need this and that," and to every request I'd say, "Yes, Bob." We'd be on the line for an hour before he realized I'd given him everything he asked for. He assembled a team of six incredibly talented people to help our hospitals organize Radiothons. Within four years that team saturated virtually every radio market in the U.S. and Canada. Listening to what they produced I would often remark, "I was watching the radio the other day" as they portrayed such vivid pictures over the airwaves. Radiothon soon became a consistent $50 million-a-year program. (**YOU GOTTA BE KIDDING!**)

The Radiothon team included Bob Lind, Karen Profita, Ken Boesen, Perry Esler, Katie Shrier, Everett Marshall, and Jim Littrell. My goodness they were amazing!

As for Champions Across America, it didn't become the press magnet I originally hoped for. The publicity was good in some places, spotty in others. We needed a full time public relations firm to manage the media campaign and we didn't have that luxury. But the impact those Miracle Kids had on everyone they came in contact with? Oh. My. Goodness. It exceeded all expectations. Having those kids front and center, in the spotlight, right where they belonged, became the emotional heart of telethon weekend.

Kids receive royal treatment from President Obama and First Lady Michelle, President Bush and First Lady Laura, and President Clinton with First Lady Hillary.

The program fit nicely with the move from Disneyland to Disney World. The Miracle Kids would fly to Ottawa and Washington, D.C. and then, after visiting the president and the prime minister, Delta and Air Canada would fly them straight down the eastern seaboard to Orlando for the telethon. The airlines made a big deal of the kids and their families. They would host a reception for them before their flight and greet them like VIPs when they landed.

At Washington and Ottawa the kids got royal treatment. Bill Clinton was in the White House when the program first started. He and First Lady Hillary Clinton (our onetime telethon host in Little Rock who received our first Children's Champion of the Year award in 1998) could not have been more supportive. The Clintons fussed over the kids like they were their own, as did George W. Bush and his wife Laura, and Barack Obama and his wife Michelle when they were in the White House. The reception with the president was always on Friday, after which the kids would go on an excursion. Some years it was to a big league baseball game (where they would be introduced), other years it might be a tour of the Capitol or a visit to a museum or the circus. Our CMN celebrities would mingle with the kids, sports stars like Drew Bledsoe and Michelle Kwan, entertainers like Amy Grant and John Rich of the country duo Big & Rich. Miss America came every year. The year John Rich came he had written a song about the Miracle Child who came from Nashville and played it for the Bushes as the young man listened. You could see the president wiping something from his eye when the song was over.

Miss America

I saw John Rich perform in the Rose Garden in person, but most years I didn't attend the White House gathering because we had a telethon to get ready for in Orlando that needed my full attention. But I was always there when the Champions arrived at Disney World on Saturday. Without fail, their entrance stopped the show. Nothing was orchestrated. But when the kids showed up, everyone rushed to them and welcomed them. And not just the Miracle Children, but their parents and their siblings, who often get neglected when the sick child in the family tends to get all the attention.

Disney World was a much bigger space for the telethon and surrounding events. By this point the weekend had grown to where each of the sponsors, after a grand welcoming event attended by all, could hold their own separate recognition luncheon or reception. The stars of these affairs were invariably the Miracle Children. They were Champions and they were treated like it. Sponsors were extremely motivated to raise more money after their experience with these Champions.

Innovations like Champions Across America and Radiothon were critical to keeping CMN evolving and expanding its reach. We were constantly on the lookout for successful fundraising campaigns that might be adapted to CMN. In late 1989 a fundraiser the students at Penn State University were doing came to our attention. They called it Dance Marathon and each year it raised in the neighborhood of $3 million for a variety of local charities, including CMN member Hershey's Medical Center in nearby Hershey, Pennsylvania.

I scheduled an appointment to fly to State College, Pennsylvania, and meet on campus with the Penn State students who were running the campaign. Because of my connections with the American Football Coaches Association, I had gotten to know Joe Paterno, the legendary Penn State football coach, who agreed to come to the start of the meeting and introduce me. If you want to know what instant credibility looks like, have Joe Pa introduce you at Penn State University.

The concept for Dance Marathon was straightforward enough: participants would dance during a twenty-one hour marathon and solicit pledges for however long they danced— like a Walkathon, but with dancing for a very long time. It was an ideal fit for college kids, and at Penn State the annual Dance Marathon had become a social event not to be missed, always attracting large crowds of students.

Over the years, the Penn State students who ran the dance marathon had refined it and turned it into quite a sophisticated operation. Not only did they recruit current students to participate, but they mailed solicitations to all previous participants. They developed a database that kept them in touch with everyone who had ever danced and made sure they knew they could still contribute. That was a powerful affinity group.

We could clearly see that Dance Marathon, Like Eleanor's Miracle Balloons, like Bob Lind's Radiothon, like Sam Walton's Workplace Fundraising, was something that could be replicated throughout the CMN world.

The Penn State organizers enthusiastically agreed to help us export what they had started. They were excited to lead the nation in expanding Dance Marathon. I took a Penn State leader with me wherever we went. We paid their expenses. It was their program and they needed to get all the credit. The first school that signed on was Indiana University, then The Ohio State University, then the University of Florida, then the University of Iowa. One by one schools committed to raising funds for their local children's hospital with Dance Marathons, until more than 150 were part of the network, collectively raising $50 million every year. (**YOU GOTTA BE KIDDING!**)

In the beginning, a number of hospital development officers were reluctant to embrace Dance Marathon. Special events tended to be expensive and labor intensive. David Gillig, chief development officer at San Diego Children's Hospital (now RADY Children's) was a Board member. He also served on the Board of the Woodmark Group. Woodmark was an organization of the premier children's hospital development officers in the country. Collaboration with them would always be invaluable. These were true leaders who put kids first.

David, hoping to build a bridge between CMN and Woodmark, conducted an in-depth review of the Dance Marathon business and financial model. He concluded that while the actual revenue generated by the event was real, the other significant opportunity Dance Marathon presented was building a database of previous dancers, many of them college grads, going out into the real world. This database of this very loyal affinity group could be solicited annually and prospected for major gifts.

MIRACLE CHILDREN:

The Bailey Brothers

"God saved the child—I just carried him."

Dennis Nielsen, a lieutenant colonel in the Iowa Air National Guard, said those words when he was praised for taking three-year-old Spencer Bailey in his arms and carrying the boy to safety from the burning wreckage of United Flight 232.

The flight had taken off from Denver, headed for Chicago, but shortly after takeoff the airplane's rear engine stopped working, causing a chain reaction of problems that included the loss of the plane's hydraulics and conventional controls. The DC-10 was a bucking bronco in the sky, with violent upward thrusts followed by severe plunges. The pilots radioed ahead to Sioux Gateway Airport in Sioux City, Iowa, the nearest possibility for an emergency landing.

Spencer Bailey had boarded the flight with his mother, Frances, and six-year-old brother Brandon (the boy's father, Brownell, and Spencer's twin brother, Trent, were not traveling with them). They were three passengers among the 296 passengers onboard Flight 232. As the airplane approached Sioux City, pilot Al Haynes warned from the cockpit: "This is gonna be the roughest landing you've ever had."

It was worse than that. The plane skidded across runway 22 and crashed in a cornfield, exploding on impact and bursting into flames.

Those nearest the blast or in the line of flying shrapnel died instantly, including Frances Bailey, one of 111 who perished that day. But the two Bailey boys were either shielded by their mother or were flung to safer areas, because when rescuers approached the plane, both were alive. Spencer, one day before his fourth birthday, was plucked out of the arms of a departing passenger by Lt. Col. Nielsen, one of several Air National Guardsmen who were on duty that day.

As Lt. Col. Nielsen carried Spencer to safety, Gary Anderson, a photographer for the Sioux City Journal, captured the dramatic image. Within hours, Anderson's photograph appeared in newspapers and on telecasts around the world. Later, it became the image for a sculpture Sioux City erected as a memorial to Flight 232, engraved with Nielsen's words: "God saved the child—I just carried him."

Spencer and Brandon Bailey were treated at St. Luke's Hospital in Sioux City and later transported to Denver Children's Hospital, where each made a full recovery. At the following year's Children's Miracle Network Telethon we invited the Bailey brothers to come to Disneyland and be honored as Miracle Kids. In a special moment after they came on stage, the audience released helium balloons into the atmosphere, in memory of their mother and the others on Flight 232 who did not make it.

Mick with Courtney Simmons

....

CHAPTER TWENTY-FIVE

Planes, Trains, and Automobiles

I was there that day.
July 19, 1989.

I was standing at the fence next to a photographer shooting video of the crash and fireball for KIVI-TV Channel 4, the CMN station in Sioux City.

I watched as United Flight 232 roared into view above the airport, preparing for a crash landing. Life is precious and very fragile. That's what I remember from that day.

I was on vacation at the time. My family and I had driven from Salt Lake City to Sioux City, the place of my birth, to visit my mother, Marjorie, and my brother, Tim. My mother was manager of a little independent motel that, as it happened, sat directly across the Missouri River from the airport. We were lounging by the motel swimming pool when Tim received a phone call alerting the Iowa State Police to respond to an emergency. He manned his patrol cruiser and sped off toward the airport. I followed in my car. Tim was in charge of the Iowa State Trooper division in northwest Iowa.

Tim was a member of the Iowa Air National Guard as well. His unit specialized in crash recovery. Any crashes, anywhere in the country, his people responded to. This one happened to be in their own backyard.

Tim was told that the airplane, a DC-10, had lost one of its tail-mounted engines and, along with that, the use of its hydraulics and many of its controls. The pilots did not think they could make it to the airport. Tim sprang to action, immediately mobilizing his Guard unit along with other first responders. In no time, seventy ambulances from all over northwest Iowa, northeast Nebraska and southeast South Dakota were racing to the Sioux City airport. I looked on as first responders lined the runway.

When United 232 came in sight it was making a series of right turns trying to get to the airport runway. It looked perfectly normal as it crossed above the Missouri River, like any other plane. But it was traveling much too fast and dropping much too quickly to do anything but skip across the runway, flip over, and touch down in the adjoining cornfield. When the plane hit it was like a bomb went off. There was a deafening explosion followed by an enormous ball of fire. I didn't think anyone could survive such a thing. Time seemed to stand still. Then, out of the haze, I watched as passengers started filing out of the cornfield. They stumbled across the runway, where enough first responders waited to offer aid and comfort to every one of them. The majority who emerged out of the cornfield required little assistance. One man walked straight into the terminal, went to the bar, had a drink, then rented a car and drove to Chicago. (It took awhile to determine that he was among the survivors.) Of the seventy ambulances, only about a dozen were needed. You either walked away from Flight 232 or you didn't. There wasn't much in between. I called my friends at KSL Radio in Salt Lake City, counting the survivors as they emerged from the cornfield. All the national newscasts led that night with the crash in Sioux City, one of the biggest aviation disasters in American history. It was the subject of a book, "Flight 232," and made into two made-for-TV movies, one starring Charlton Heston and Richard Thomas.

The crash turned personal when I learned that four of our CMN hospital directors were on board. They were returning from a national meeting in Denver, attended by about four hundred of our directors, on their way to Chicago when the plane crashed in Sioux City. I didn't know about the four CMN directors until Steve Williams called from our office in Salt Lake City and told me the news. I looked for their names back at the motel my mother managed. It had been turned over to United as a crisis center. The airline put up a big board that listed all the passengers and their status. I was relieved to see that three of our people were safe. I was able to locate them at the hospital and drive them to the airport to catch the plane TWA had loaned to United to get its passengers to Chicago. The fourth, made it to St. Luke's Hospital in Sioux City but her injuries were too severe and months later she passed on. Her mother and father and her husband were flown in by United. They were first taken into a room where the head nurse prepared them for what they were about to see. Elaine's husband was a big man, well over six feet tall; he passed out when he first saw his wife, still clinging to life.

I traveled over three million air miles during my twenty-eight years as CEO of Children's Miracle Network, 2.8 million of them on one airline: Delta (and Western before the merge.) I was fortunate to fly all those miles, and visit all those hospitals and sponsors, without serious mishap or concern.

But that much flying is not without adventure. One time Joe and I were in New York when a snowstorm hit the city. A grand total of two inches had fallen. That was enough to shut down Kennedy Airport. The Western flight coming to Kennedy from Salt Lake was diverted to Laguardia Airport, where it let off its passengers. That meant that evening's return flight from Kennedy to Salt Lake was canceled. We've all been there, done that. The passengers were disgruntled and grumpy, giving the gate agents a hard time. Joe and I, being very familiar with those gate agents, went out and bought all three of them a box of candy. We then spent the night at the Kennedy Airport Marriott. The next morning, as Kennedy reopened, the FAA would not allow the aircraft to ferry from Laguardia to Kennedy. Thus the passengers would be spending all day at Kennedy waiting for the evening flight back to Salt Lake. The aircraft at Laguardia would be deadheaded back to Salt Lake City to stay in the system, without any passengers on board. Joe and I were stranded at Kennedy with the rest of the passengers. We had worked with Jim Dimagio, Western's station manager at Kennedy, over the years. He caught our eye. "You guys probably want to get back to Salt Lake, right?" he said. "Well, grab your bags and come with me."

We got in his pickup, he drove us to LaGuardia, and we would dead head back to Salt Lake with just the crew and Joe and me on that plane.

On another Western trip, this one from Salt Lake to Chicago, the flight was full, not a seat to be had, when we got to the gate, which sometimes happened because of overbooking. Recognizing me as a non-revenue frequent flyer, the gate agent called me over and said he'd take care of me by putting me in a jump seat in the cockpit. We were flying over Iowa when the pilot turned and asked, "So what do you do with Western?" "Nothing," I said. "Why are you up here?" he said. "The gate agent put me here," I answered. "Don't ever tell anybody about this, I'll get thirty days off, without pay," said the pilot. I wasn't supposed to be there. Neither of us knew what that gate agent was thinking, but I got to Chicago on time.

Another time I was stranded by weather when a storm canceled all flights out of Cedar Rapids, Iowa, where I'd had a meeting at the University of Iowa Children's Hospital. When I arrived the terminal was empty, as all the passengers had been bused to the Greyhound station. Two Midway Airline mechanics were standing at the counter. I approached them, confirming that I had no options to fly out of Cedar Rapids. With just the three of us in the empty terminal, one of them mentioned that they were flying a small Midway plane to Des Moines to get the radio repaired. Right out of Petticoat Junction, one of them said, "Come on, we'll take you over." I jumped at the opportunity, failing to carefully factor in that part about the radio not working. Once we were in the air, without a radio, they veered off track. All they had to do was follow I-80. They were attempting to figure out where Des Moines was. Out the right side of the window I saw the Iowa State University and the football stadium, which is directly north of Des Moines. I said, "Hey guys, hang a left and follow the freeway to Des Moines. When you get to I-80 hang another left and the airport's right there. We found the airport and I was able to get a flight to Salt Lake. All in a day's work.

You meet interesting people when you're held captive in an airplane. On one flight I found myself in a middle seat between Merrill Osmond in the window seat. Merrill fell asleep against the window, snoring away. Adrian Dantley, the future Hall of Fame basketball star who played at the time for the Utah Jazz, was on the aisle. He was very intently working on his monthly budget with a yellow legal pad. I found it intriguing. He had over thirty line items on his monthly budget. It totaled $750 a month. Here's an NBA all-star on a $750 a month budget! A.D.'s wife was an attorney in Chicago and obviously had him on a tight leash.

One of the more harrowing experience came on a flight to Hawaii with Utah Jazz basketball star Thurl Bailey and his wife, Sindi. We were flying to the annual Ace Hardware celebrity golf tournament held every year on the Big Island. The first tip that it wasn't going to be smooth sailing was when the Delta plane we boarded in Salt Lake caught on fire and had to make an emergency landing in San Francisco. Hours later, Delta replaced the plane and we continued to Honolulu. The delay meant we had missed our connecting flight to the Big Island. The airport was shut down. It seemed we would have to spend the night in Honolulu and try to fly out the next morning. But as we collected our bags, I noticed that one counter was still lit up. It was a scenic flight operator. As we walked by, I just casually asked if they might have the ability to fly us over to the Big Island. There were four of us and they indicated that for $200 each they would fly us over. However, as we were approaching the little tiny plane, Sindi Bailey punched Thurl in the shoulder and said, "Thurl I'm not getting on that plane. You take me downtown and get me a hotel right now!" So, there we stand, ready to head for the Big Island, Sindi determined she's not going to get on that little airplane and fly over the ocean. I said, "Come on, Sindi, you won't have to pedal. I'll do all the pedaling." She acquiesced and we boarded the plane, and did not die that night on that flight to the Big Island.

All flights were good flights that landed safely (and preferably in the right city.) One night, on a flight from Salt Lake to Las Vegas, the pilot came on the intercom. "Just so y'all know," he drawled. "It takes a lot of training to be a pilot these days. If you folks on the right side of the airplane would look out your window you'll see a red blinking light out there. And it's interesting, but if you folks on the left side of the airplane look out your window you'll see a red blinking light out there. I've learned in my training all I have to do is keep this airplane between those two red blinking lights and I'm going to get y'all to Las Vegas."

Three million miles generates a lot of stories. On a flight from Salt Lake to San Francisco we had a fun experience. As we were flying in over the bay to land, just before we were to touch down the pilot put the pedal to the metal and we climbed quickly back up over the airport. The pilot made an announcement that some knucklehead in a small plane had just crossed our runway. "If I had hit him you wouldn't even have felt it. I did get his tail number and he's going to pay for 5,000 pounds of fuel."

MIRACLE CHILD:

ANJELA UHLENKOTT

For nearly thirty minutes, after four-year-old Anjela Uhlenkott of Asotin, Washington, steered her tricycle into the family swimming pool, nothing happened. Anjee just lay there at the bottom, motionless, unable to breathe.

Robin Roberts, host of *Good Morning America*, and
Anjela Uhlenkott

But when her family discovered where she was and what had happened, heaven and earth moved. In a stupefying human chain reaction nothing short of miraculous, Anjee was brought back to life.

It began when her mother, Deb, discovered Anjee in the swimming pool. Her father, Ron, jumped in and pulled her out. Her sister, Alexis, called 911. A family friend, Pat Greenfield, fortuitously heard about the "drowning" on her police scanner and called pediatrician Craig Ambroson to see if he could do anything to help.

Dr. Ambroson lived near the Uhlenkotts. He got in his car and quickly drove to their home, getting there before the ambulance paramedics arrived. He immediately took over CPR procedures and authorized the administration of epinephrine and atropine to get Anjee's heart beating again, saving precious minutes when none could be spared.

By the time Anjee arrived at **St. Joseph's Hospital** in Lewiston, Idaho, a helicopter was already on its way from Spokane to fly her to the **Sacred Heart Medical Center**. At Sacred Heart, doctors attached Anjee to an oscillating ventilator to keep her heart beating and put her into a drug-induced coma to keep the swelling down and allow the brain to recover. None at this point were overly optimistic, but all were hopeful.

All they could do was wait.

A long week later, doctors told Deb and Ron: "I think you're going to get your daughter back."

As she emerged out of her coma, Anjee couldn't talk, walk, eat, or swallow. But she could breathe and there were no signs of permanent brain damage. She got to start life all over again. With the assistance of numerous therapists and tireless hours of rehabilitation, her recovery proceeded unimpeded. By the time she was six she was laughing and running and riding her bike—and trying out for the local swim team.

Medically, it was hard to explain how a little girl who had been at the bottom of a swimming pool for nearly half-an-hour could recover so fully. But no one doubted that the timely actions of so many caring people made it at least a possibility.

"All the prayers that went up with her when she left in the helicopter were answered," said Dr. Ambroson. "I believe God has some special plans for Anjela."

In 1998, shortly after she tried out for the swim team, Anjela Uhlenkott was flown to Orlando as a CMN Champion. There, she was able to meet and have her picture taken with sports broadcaster Robin Roberts, a loyal CMN celebrity supporter who years later would herself inspire many with her courageous battle with cancer.

Staff photo 1995 Telethon

....

CHAPTER TWENTY-SIX

Always Hire People Smarter than You

They made me look good every day. They made sure everything we did passed the test of **Always putting kids first.**

The legendary Hall of Fame football coach at BYU once told me, "... Always hire people smarter than you. For some of us, that's easier than others." Obviously, that was very easy for me.

From the beginning, that was the guiding principle for Children's Miracle Network—the mantra that got us started and kept us going. And from the beginning, a dedicated staff made sure we stayed true to that mission. People came for the job and stayed for the passion. Our corporate sponsors would constantly rave about our staff: *Where do you find these people? ... wish we could find people like that.* But the truth was, we didn't find them as much as they found us. And once they came, they tended not to leave. It's remarkable how many early hires were still with us more than three decades later.

Management and staff started out few in number and by design stayed that way. Our story was always about how small our staff was, not how big it was. CMN experienced exponential growth in its first five years, expanding from twenty-two member hospitals in 1983 to one hundred and forty-two in 1987, with one hundred and seventy-four television stations broadcasting the telethon compared to thirty stations in 1983. All of it was administered by just twenty-seven people. The following is a list of that lean and mean pioneering staff of twenty-seven:

Management team: Jay Vestal, vice president of marketing; Scott Burt, vice president of finance; Steve Williams, public relations director; Gary Swenson, vice president of field operations; Thomas Abbott, vice president of special events.

Regional directors: Cary Miller, southeastern region; Susan Roady, northeastern region; Doug Nielsen, western region; Stephanie Melemis, Canadian region; Susan Sulsky, midwestern region.

Staff members: Pat Howell, executive secretary; Laurie England, administrative assistant, marketing; Renae Finlayson, director of internal communications and telethon operations; Ellen Johansen, public relations assistant; Janice O'Hern, administrative assistant, northeastern region; Patricia Parker, administrative assistant, southeastern region; Rebecca Davis, accounts manager; Cindy Hopkins, administrative assistant, western region; Bonnie Polgar, administrative assistant, midwestern region; Susan Goodale, administrative assistant, Canadian region; Max Burdick, Jr., account executive; Kathy Brinton, secretary, field operations; Maury Christensen, communications specialist; Shannon Hill, secretary, special events; Jana Clarke, secretary, marketing; Carla Barlow, receptionist; Randall Beckham, administrative assistant.

As the organization continued to grow, for decades we never exceeded fifty people on staff. We weren't raising money for ourselves, we were raising money for the kids. Everybody wore more than one hat. Each had their daily jobs and daily routines but when it came time for the telethon they all had additional responsibilities putting it together. They were passionate about the kids and loved their jobs and worked so hard and made all of us look good with the work product they put out—never losing the vision of the kids being first.

The people behind the curtain truly made the difference, allowing the crazy idea Joe and I created out of thin air to acquire form and substance and respectability. In those early formative years, bringing in people with skills and expertise we didn't have enabled the organization to turn the corner and begin to prosper. People like fundraiser extraordinaire Jay Vestal, our first professional hire. Jay personified the type of person attracted by the mission more than the salary. He agreed to move to Utah from Little Rock, where he had an excellent job with Arkansas Children's Hospital, strictly because of his passion for kids and his vision of what CMN could accomplish. He took a pay cut to come. His input proved to be beyond critical. Jay's leadership in creating Cause Marketing opportunities in the early years was the biggest reason CMN was able to pay its bills and stay alive.

We brought in Steve Williams from the IHC hospital in Idaho Falls. Steve was a master of communications. He knew branding inside and out; an absolute genius. When Steve left, his replacement, Craig Sorensen, took over communications without missing a beat. Roger Cook came to us from Rogers & Cowan, the gigantic entertainment management agency in Los Angeles. Roger was amazing at event management, as was Renae Finlayson.

Stephanie Melemis was invaluable in helping CMN establish meaningful roots in Canada. She oversaw the CMN program directors at the CMN network hospitals in Canada, inspiring all with her enthusiasm and passion. After Stephanie passed away, CMN created the Stephanie Melemis Excellence in Service Award, an honor given every year in Orlando to a program director for demonstrating superior service in fundraising and raising awareness for the CMN cause.

Cynthia Nay, Kathy Anderson, and Ida Fadden were just a few of the office assistants who made Joe and me look like we might know what we were doing. Pat Howell was our very dependable, reliable, always-there executive assistant who handled both Joe and me at the same time, if you can imagine that.

Wally Edwards became a jack of all trades, seeing all sides of the operation. Now thirty years later, he's in a senior management position.

Shirley Rogers came to us from Marriott Corporate. She set up an HR department the way it should be set up, with documentation, record-keeping, and a specified chain of command. The Board of Trustees was thrilled when they saw her professionalism and organization, as they were when we brought in Scott Burt as Chief Financial Officer. Scott was a true professional of unparalleled integrity who formalized our accounting processes and reporting procedures so there was never any question about finances. I was no longer guessing with regard to our budget, expenses, and revenues. (But I was the best doggone guesser you'll ever find.)

These dedicated people, and so many, many more, formed the heart of CMN. **I learned from them every day.** My management philosophy was to delegate and get out of their way and let them do what they did best. That left me free to do what I did best: hitting the road and telling the CMN story with a passion. I was the rainmaker, as Scott Burt once put it. Because of everyone else doing their job, and doing it so very well, I was able to foster relationships with big partners, like Dairy Queen, Walmart, Costco, McLane, ACE, and RE/MAX, that kept us viable and always growing and moving forward. I did not manage anything. I didn't have to. I left that to people a lot smarter than me.

When my time came to step down as head of the organization and turn the reins over to someone else, the hardest part was leaving the people—so many individuals who have my undying respect and admiration.

They were all class in sending me off, giving me far more praise than I deserved. I'll always treasure their comments:

From Marie Osmond: "It has been a privilege to work so closely with Mick Shannon and help build Children's Miracle Network to what it is today. Mick's inspiration, dedication, and creativity have taken Children's Miracle Network to heights that none of us could have ever imagined."

From John Schneider: "Being a part of this network of good that Mick Shannon has created is an honor for me, but also a great blessing for millions of kids throughout North America. Mick is not only a leader, he's a friend, an inspiration, and a hero."

From Joe Lake: "Mick is one of the smartest and most creative men I know. I know that as much as Mick cares for kids, his own and all the kids, he will sleep well at night knowing that he has made a major impact on the lives of kids, yesterday, today, and tomorrow."

From Drayton McLane, Chairman, McLane Group: 'Few people get to make a great difference in the lives of so many, and Mick has had such a positive impact on thousands of people. Thanks for setting a tremendous example, and building something with great integrity and leadership."

From Brett Hutchens, President, Casto Lifestyle Properties: "Mick Shannon has always safeguarded the fundamental principles of Children's Miracle Network and measures all his decisions in the context of 'Will this help the kids?'"

From Mario Pilozzi, President and CEO, Walmart Canada Corp.: "Mick Shannon's passion shaped an unwavering vision for Children's Miracle Network, and his determination propelled it into one of North America's biggest forces for good. Mick is an inspiration to me and Walmart associates across the continent, who believe in the power of good works."

From Steve Weisz, President, Marriott Vacation Club International: "The results of Mick Shannon's efforts are obvious—the finest, most successful charitable organization in North America! He can depart knowing that the flame that was started over 22 years ago by he and Joe burns brightly in all of us that he leaves behind."

From Carolynn A. Bond, Director Community Affairs and Liaison to Children's Miracle Network, RE/MAX International, Inc.: "I am so touched by Mick's humility and true interest in serving children. That quality has helped this organization stay its course."

From Jimmy Alexander, VP Human Resources, Ace Hardware Corporation: "To accomplish great things a leader must not only act, but also dream; not only plan, but also believe. Mick, thank you for believing, dreaming, and leading Children's Miracle Network to tremendous heights."

From Rick Bucciarelli, MD, Associate Vice President for Health Affairs for Government Relations, University of Florida: "Mick Shannon, through his vision, has achieved an international level of impact shared by very few and now through his legacy will continue to have an increasing impact for decades to come! A truly remarkable accomplishment!"

MIRACLE CHILD:

Courtney Simmons

From Miracle Child to Miracle Worker. From cancer survivor to CMN fundraiser. That's the path Court Simmons took as she transformed from a cancer patient at Children's Hospital of Philadelphia to executive director of the Dance Marathon at St. Joseph's University in Philadelphia.

Court's childhood was anything but easy. She was nine years old when her mother Crystal was first diagnosed with cancer. She was twelve when her sister Christina died of a cancerous brain tumor. And she had just turned sixteen when her mother died from the cancer she had been battling.

That's the same year Court was diagnosed with a rare type of cancer called osteocarsoma that appeared in her left leg. With only her fourteen-year-old brother Reginald left in her family and no legal guardian, Court began chemotherapy treatments at **Children's Hospital of Philadelphia**. The nurses and doctors took her under their wing, caring for her as if she were their own child. After months of chemo, the tumor in her left leg bone had shrunk to the point it could be removed by surgery. Court was given a titanium knee replacement and a titanium femur prosthesis, requiring months of rehab as she had to learn to walk all over again.

Finally, in the fall of 2012 she was able to leave the hospital and return for her senior year of high school, where through persistence and perseverance she graduated on time with her class. She received a full-tuition cancer survivor's scholarship to St. Joseph's, enabling her to pursue her dream of becoming a nurse.

Once she had her feet on the ground at college, she learned about the Dance Marathon put on by St. Joseph's students to benefit CMN member Children's Hospital of Philadelphia—her home away from home for the many weeks and months she battled cancer.

She couldn't NOT sign up as a volunteer.

Before she knew it, she was the woman in charge. In her junior and senior years, 2016 and 2017, she became executive director of St. Joseph's Dance Marathon, overseeing the myriad of details that go into producing a successful event.

"When I finished cancer treatment in 2012 I had a burning desire to give something to my Children's Miracle Network hospital in exchange for saving my life," Court said in explaining her desire to get involved. "Dance Marathon gave me the opportunity to tangibly support the hospital."

She listed all the reasons children's hospitals deserve everyone's support.

"People should donate to their local CMN Hospitals because it's one of the best places you can invest your money," she said. "If that's not enough, donate because the person in the hospital receiving a cancer diagnosis did not ever think this would happen to them the previous day. No person wants this for a child. Because of donations to my children's hospital, I was able to have one of the best children's hospitals in the nation twenty minutes from my home. Because of those donations, I was able to Skype into my classroom with a computer provided by the hospital and graduate on time. That computer was the resource for avoiding a delayed graduation due to my diagnosis. Because of those dollars, I was able to dream. I live and breathe Dance Marathon so all kids can have the resources to dream, regardless of having to be in the hospital."

For Court, it was personal. For the first Dance Marathon she was in charge of, the students set a goal of raising $18,510—a symbolic number reflecting the year St. Joseph's began in 1851. They raised $27,000. The next year they raised even more.

John Lauck, President and CEO of Children's Miracle Network Hospitals

....

CHAPTER TWENTY-SEVEN

CMNH Today

From its start in 1983 through 2018, for thirty-six consecutive years, Children's Miracle Network raised more money each year for children's hospitals than the previous year. I know of no other charity that can make such a claim. During my time as CEO, the lowest annual growth rate we ever had was nine percent, and we were upset the one year when we didn't hit double digits!

From $4.7 million collected in 1983 to the $400 million collected in 2018, CMN had to that point raised nearly $7 billion for children's hospitals, and counting—not bad for an organization that began with nothing but a credit card and a dream.

Equally significant and impressive is this fact: Children's Miracle Network has consistently been given four stars—the highest rating possible—by Charity Navigator, America's largest independent charity evaluator. The founding principle of **HAVING THE LOWEST COST RATIO AMONG NON-PROFITS** has been faithfully adhered to.

CMN's hallmark has been the ability to evolve and change with the times. The best evidence of that is the demise of the telethon. The final CMN Telethon was aired at Disney World in 2012. It marked the end of an era, as all national telethons were being rendered obsolete due to changing viewer habits and the proliferation of cable television and online streaming services. No longer did the big three television networks command a lion's share of the national viewing audience, nor did marathon singing-and-dancing extravaganzas have the appeal they once had. (The Jerry Lewis MDA Labor Day Telethon ended its long run in 2014, but was shortened to just a two-hour special its final three years. Other long-running national telethons had phased out earlier than that.)

Think of that. The very vehicle that had paved the way for CMN's existence, its signature event for thirty years, went the way of the dinosaurs—and yet the organization did not miss a beat. Sponsors remained. Donations continued to increase. Telethon Weekend was replaced by four days of festivities in Orlando at Disney World—**Children's Hospital Week,** a celebration of everything associated with helping sick kids get better. This was a brilliant move by John Lauck and his amazing team.

As with the CMN Telethon, Children's Hospital Week gives corporate sponsors the opportunity to mingle with Miracle Children and identify who it is they are helping and why. The week allows the sponsors to step up and be recognized for their fundraising efforts, then and now. The loyalty and staying power of CMN's corporate sponsors is nothing short of legendary.

Innovation continues to keep CMN viable and fresh. Among the biggest innovations in the twenty-first century is a program that would have been unthinkable in 1983—unthinkable because the technology hadn't yet been invented to make it possible. It's called Extra Life and involves video gamers. Gaming enthusiasts solicit pledges from friends, family members, and fellow gamers for playing a certain amount of games on a certain day. "Raise funds, have fun, and help heal kids at your local Children's Miracle Network Hospital," is how it's explained at extra-life.org, the fundraiser's website (Something else unimaginable in 1983.) Through their "gaming marathons," Extra Life gamers have collectively raised more than $50 million since the program began in 2008.

Dance Marathon continues to be a huge fundraising vehicle for CMN. What began in 1989 with students at Penn State University raising money for Hershey's Medical Center has ballooned into more than 300 Dance Marathons at colleges and high schools throughout North America, each raising funds for the local children's hospital down the street. For periods of twenty-four hours or even longer, Dance Marathon participants collect pledges by dancing, playing games, and celebrating with Miracle Kids from the hospitals. In 2018 alone Dance Marathons raised more than $50 million, and all told have collected more than $250 million.

Leading the way into the future is CEO John Lauck, a capable leader brought in from the private sector. John was CEO at Mrs. Fields Cookies when recruiters approached him about taking over the reins at CMN in 2011. At first he showed no interest, knowing virtually nothing about nonprofits or children's hospitals and fundraising. He had made his mark as a manager and marketer in the for-profit business world, serving in senior marketing roles at PepsiCo/Pizza Hut, General Mills, Blockbuster, and Footaction.

But his mind was changed when he opened the packet of materials the recruiters sent him and played a DVD that was enclosed. The DVD was full of miracle stories—tales of sick kids who got better at children's hospitals.

"I was emotionally moved by these incredible stories. I wasn't expecting that," said Lauck. "Not one thing I'd done had made the world any better. But here I could make a difference."

So he took the job.

I could relate. Years ago, when I drove the little orange Toyota to Idaho, I had no appreciation for what was about to grab hold of me and not let go.

Like so many before John Lauck, and so many yet to come, it was the kids who made all the difference.

Afterword

When Andy Andrews, the bestselling author and great friend to Children's Miracle Network, finished his book *Miracles One at A Time*, he sent me a copy hot off the presses. I opened to a page near the front and read a quote that hit me right between the eyes:

> **"** Our deepest fear is not that we are inadequate. Our deepest fear is that we are powerful beyond measure. It is our light, not our darkness that most frightens us. We ask ourselves, 'Who am I to be brilliant, gorgeous, talented, fabulous?' Actually, who are you not to be? You are a child of God. Your playing small does not serve the world. There is nothing enlightened about shrinking so that other people won't feel insecure around you. We are all meant to shine, as children do. We were born to make manifest the glory of God that is within us. It's not just in some of us; it's in everyone. And as we let our own light shine, we unconsciously give other people permission to do the same. As we are liberated from our own fear, our presence automatically liberates others. **"**

The words stopped me in my tracks. (They were written by a writer named Marianne Williamson, although they are often ascribed to Nelson Mandela, who said something similar in his 1994 inaugural address in South Africa.) They personified all of the people who had made—and continue to make—CMN a success! People at every turn who did not play small, who were powerful beyond measure. That includes everybody in this book. From John and Marie, to the kids, to the entertainers, to the sponsors, to the doctors and nurses, and anyone and everyone in between. They all played big. They all served the world. They all let their light shine bright. It's been the great blessing of my life to stand back and watch the tremendous miracles they have made happen. And repeatedly shake my head in amazement. **YOU GOTTA BE KIDDING!**

Appendix

NETWORK HOSPITALS
affiliated with Children's Miracle Network

USA

Alabama:	Children's of Alabama
	University of South Alabama Children's & Women's Hospital
Alaska:	The Children's Hospital at Providence
Arizona:	Phoenix Children's Hospital
	Tucson Medical Center
Arkansas:	Arkansas Children's Hospital
California:	Children's Hospital Central California
	Children's Hospital Los Angeles
	Children's Hospital & Research Center Oakland
	CHOC Children's
	Cottage Children's Hospital
	Lauren Small Children's Medical Center at Bakersfield Memorial Hospital

	Rady Children's Hospital-San Diego
	Salinas Valley Memorial Hospital
	UC Davis Children's Hospital
Colorado:	Children's Hospital Colorado
Connecticut:	Connecticut Children's Medical Center
District of Columbia:	Children's National Medical Center
Florida:	All Children's Hospital
	Arnold Palmer Children's Hospital
	Miami Children's Hospital (Now Jack Nicklaus Children's Hospital)
	Sacred Heart Children's Hospital
	Shands Hospital for Children at the University of Florida
	UF & Shands Jacksonville
	Wolfson Children's Hospital
Georgia:	Children's Healthcare of Atlanta
	Children's Hospital at Memorial University Medical Center
	Children's Hospital of Georgia
	Phoebe Putney Memorial Hospital
	The Children's Hospital at the Medical Center of Central Georgia
	The Medical Center
Hawaii:	Kapi'olani Medical Center for Women & Children
Idaho:	Kootenai Medical Center
	St. Luke's Children's Hospital
Illinois:	Ann & Robert H. Lurie Children's Hospital of Chicago
	Children's Hospital of Illinois
	St. John's Children's Hospital
Indiana:	Riley Hospital for Children

Iowa:	Unity Point Health – St. Luke's
	University of Iowa Children's Hospital
Kansas:	KU Medical Center
	St. Francis Health Center
	Via Christi Hospitals in Wichita
Kentucky:	Kentucky Children's Hospital
	Kosair Children's Hospital
Louisiana:	Children's Hospital – New Orleans
	CHRISTUS Health Shreveport-Bossier
	CHRISTUS St. Frances Cabrini Hospital
	CHRISTUS St. Patrick Hospital
	Our Lady of the Lake Children's Hospital
Maine:	Blue Hill Memorial Hospital
	C.A. Dean Memorial Hospital
	Eastern Maine Medical Center
	Sebasticook Valley Hospital
	The Acadia Hospital
	The Aroostook Medical Center
	The Barbara Bush Children's Hospital at Maine Medical Center
Maryland:	Johns Hopkins Children's Center
Massachusetts:	Baystate Children's Hospital
	Boston Children's Hospital
Michigan:	Beaumont Children's Hospital
	Helen DeVos Children's Hospital
	Hurley Children's Hospital
	Sparrow Hospital
Minnesota:	Gillette Children's Specialty Healthcare
Mississippi:	Blair E. Batson Children's Hospital at the University of MississippiMedical Center
Missouri:	Cardinal Glennon Children's Medical Center

	CoxHealth
	Freeman Health System
	MU Children's Hospital
	St. Louis Children's Hospital
Montana:	Shodair Children's Hospital
Nebraska:	Children's Hospital & Medical Center
Nevada:	Renown Children's Hospital
	St. Rose Dominican Hospitals
New Jersey:	Children's Specialized Hospital
New Mexico:	UNM Children's Hospital
New York:	Arnot Ogden Medical Center
	Children's Hospital at Albany Medical Center
	Faxton-St. Luke's Healthcare
	Golisano Children's Hospital at the University of Rochester Medical Center
	Maria Fareri Children's Hospital at Westchester Medical Center
	Samaritan Medical Center
	Steven and Alexandra Cohen Children's Medical Center of New York
	Upstate Golisano Children's Hospital
	Women & Children's Hospital of Buffalo
North Carolina:	Duke Children's Hospital & Health Center
	Levine Children's Hospital
	James and Connie Maynard Children's Hospital at Vidant Medical Center
North Dakota:	Sanford Children's Hospital
Ohio:	Akron Children's Hospital
	Cincinnati Children's Hospital Medical Center
	Mercy Children's Hospital
	Nationwide Children's Hospital

	The Children's Medical Center
	University Hospitals Rainbow Babies & Children's Hospital
Oklahoma:	Children's Hospital Foundation
	The Children's Hospital at Saint Francis
Oregon:	Asante Rogue Regional Medical Center
	Asante Three Rivers Medical Center
	OHSU Doernbecher Children's Hospital
	PeaceHealth Sacred Heart Medical Center
Pennsylvania:	Children's Hospital of Pittsburgh of UPMC
	Penn State Children's Hospital at Penn State Milton S. Hershey Medical Center
	Saint Vincent Health Center
	The Children's Hospital of Philadelphia
	The Janet Weis Children's Hospital at Geisinger
Puerto Rico:	San Jorge Children's Foundation
Rhode Island:	Hasbro Children's Hospital
South Carolina:	Greenville Health System
	McLeod Children's Hospital
	Medical University of South Carolina Children's Hospital
	Palmetto Health Children's Hospital
South Dakota:	Rapid City Regional Hospital
	Sanford Health USD Medical Center
Tennessee:	Children's Hospital at Erlanger
	East Tennessee Children's Hospital
	Le Bonheur Children's Hospital
	Monroe Carell Jr. Children's Hospital at Vanderbilt
	Wellmont Health System
Texas:	Children's Hospital of San Antonio

Children's Medical Center

CHRISTUS Hospital – St. Elizabeth

CHRISTUS Hospital – St. Mary

CHRISTUS Jasper Memorial Hospital

Cook Children's Medical Center

Dell Children's Medical Center of Central Texas

Driscoll Children's Hospital

Harrington Cancer Foundation

Hendrick Medical Center

McLane Children's Hospital Scott & White

Medical Center Health System Foundation

Mother Frances Hospital

Shannon Medical Center

Texas Children's Hospital

UMC Children's Hospital

United Regional Health Care System

University Medical Center Foundation of El Paso

Utah: Primary Children's Hospital

Vermont: Vermont Children's Hospital at Fletcher Allen Health Care

Virginia: Carilion Clinic Children's Hospital

Centra Lynchburg General and Virginia Baptist Hospitals

Children's Hospital of Richmond at VCU

Children's Hospital of The King's Daughters

University of Virginia Children's Hospital

Washington: Inland Northwest Health Services

Providence Holy Family Hospital

Providence Mount Carmel Hospital

	Providence St. Joseph's Hospital
	Sacred Heart Children's Hospital
	Seattle Children's Hospital
	St. Luke's Rehabilitation Institute
	Yakima Valley Memorial Hospital
West Virginia:	West Virginia University Children's Hospital
Wisconsin:	Children's Hospital of Wisconsin
	Gundersen Health System
	Ministry Saint Joseph's Children's Hospital

CANADA

Calgary – Southern Alberta:
Alberta Children's Hospital Foundation

Edmonton – Northern Alberta:
Stollery Children's Hospital Foundation

Halifax, NS – Maritimes:
IWK Health Centre Foundation

Hamilton – Ontario:
McMaster Children's Hospital Foundation

London – Western Ontario:
Children's Health Foundation

Manitoba:
Children's Hospital Foundation of Manitoba

Newfoundland & Labrador:
Janeway Children's Hospital Foundation

Ottawa – Eastern Ontario:
Children's Hospital of Eastern Ontario Foundation

Saskatchewan:
Children's Hospital Foundation of Saskatchewan

Toronto–North & Central Ontario:
SickKids

Vancouver – Province of BC:
BC Children's Hospital Foundation

TELEVISION STATIONS
affiliated with Children's Miracle Network
Listed by market size:

New York:
WOR-IND

Los Angeles:
KHJ-IND

Chicago:
WLS-ABC

Philadelphia:
CN8-CAB

San Francisco-Oakland-San Jose:
KGO-ABC

Boston:
WSBK-UPN

Dallas-Ft. Worth:
KTVT-CBS, KTXA-UPN

Washington, D.C.:
WUSA-CBS

Detroit:
WKPD-UPN

Atlanta:
WGCL-CBS

Houston:
KHOU-CBS

Seattle-Tacoma:
KAPP-ABC, KOMO-ABC

Akron:
WMFD-IND, WVPX-PAX

Cleveland:
WEWS-ABC

Tampa-St. Petersburg-Sarasota:
WFLA-NBC, WTVK-UPN

Minneapolis-St. Paul:
KSTP-ABC, KMSP

Miami-Ft. Lauderdale:
WBFS-UPN

Phoenix:
KTVKL-IND

Denver:
KWGN-WB

Pittsburgh:
KDKA-CBS

Sacramento-Stockton-Modesto:
KCRA-NBC, KQCA-WB

St. Louis:
KBSI-FOX, KPLR-WB, WDKA-WB

Orlando:
WKMG-CBS

Portland, OR:
KATU-ABC

Baltimore:
WMAR-ABC

Indianapolis:
WPTA-FOX, WTHI-CBS, WTHR-NBC, WTVW-FOX

San Diego:
KGTV-ABC

Hartford-New Haven:
WTIC-FOX

Charlotte:
WCNC-NBC

Raleigh-Durham:
WGPX-PAX, WRAL-CBS, WWAY-ABC

Nashville:
WTVF-CBS

Milwaukee:
CABLE

Cincinnati:
WKRC-CBS

Kansas City:
KCTV-CBS

Columbus, OHIO:
WBNS-CBS

Greenville-Spartanburg-Asheville-Anderson:
WYFF-NBC

Salt Lake City:
KIDK-CBS, KSL-NBC

San Antonio:
WOAI-NBC

Grand Rapids-Kalamazoo-Battle Creek:
WOOD-NBC, WSTU/WQTQ-ABC

Birmingham:
WAAY-ABC, WSFA-NBC, WTVY-CBS, WVTM-NBC

Norfolk-Portsmouth-Newport News:
WVEC-ABC

New Orleans:
WDSU-NBC

Memphis:
WABG-ABC, WCBI-CBS, WREG-CBS

Oklahoma City:
KOCO-ABC

Harrisburg-Lancaster-Lebanon-York:
WGAL-NBC

Albuquerque-Santa Fe:
KRPV-IND

Wiles Barre-Scranton:
WBNG-CBS, WTAJ-CBS, WYOU-CBS

Albany-Schenectady-Troy:
WXXA

Dayton:
WHIO-CBS

Fresno-Visilia:
KFSN-ABC

Las Vegas:
KTNV-ABC

Little Rock-Pine Bluff:
KAIT-ABC, KFAA-NBC, KTHV-CBS, KTVE-NBC

Charleston-Huntington:
WDTV-CBS, WOWK-CBS, WTOV-NBC

Tulsa:
KJRH

Austin:
KEYE

Richmond-Petersburg:
WWBT-NBC

Mobile:
FOX-10-FOX

Pensacola:
WEAR-ABC, WMBB-ABC

Knoxville:
WBIR-NBC

Flint-Saginaw-Bay City:
WJRT-ABC

Wichita-Hutchinson Plus:
KSNW-NBC

Toledo:
WUPW-FOX

Lexington:
WKYT-CBS

Roanoke-Lynchburg:
WSET-ABC

Green Bay-Appleton:
CABLE

Honolulu:
OC

Spokane:
KXLY-ABC

Omaha:
KHAS-NBC, WOWT-NBC

Syracuse:
WIXT-ABC

Rochester, NY:
WHEC-NBC

Tucson:
KTTU-UPN

Springfield, MO:
KYTV-NBC

Portland-Auburn:
WGME-CBS

Champaign-Springfield-Decatur:
WICD-NBC, WICS-NBC

Columbia, SC:
WIS-NBC

Chattanooga:
WTVC-ABC

Cedar Rapids-Waterloo-Dubuque:
MEDIACOM

Jackson, MS:
WJTV-CBS

Burlington-Plattsburgh:
WCAX-CBS

Tri Cities, TN-VA:
WJHL-CBS

Waco-Temple-Bryan:
KCEN-NBC

Youngstown:
WFMJ-NBC

Baton Rouge:
WBRZ-ABC

El Paso:
KVIA-ABC

Savannah:
WTOC-CBS

Springfield-Holyoke:
WWLP-NBC

Greenville-New Bern-Washington:
WITN-NBC

Lansing:
WILX-NBC

Tyler-Longview (Tufkin &
Nacogdoches):
KETK-NBC

Reno:
KOLO-ABC

Sioux Falls (Mitchell):
KELO-CBS

Peoria-Bloomington:
WEEK-NBC

Augusta:
WRDW-CBS

Florence-Myrtle Beach:
WBTW-CBS

Fargo-Valley City:
KFYR-NBC, KMOT-NBC, KQCD-
NBC, KUMV-NBC, KVLY-NBC

Santa Barbara-Santa Maria-San
Luis Obispo:
KEYT-ABC

Monterey-Salinas:
KSBW-NBC, COMCAST

Charleston, SC:
WCSC-CBS

Eugene:
KEZI-ABC

Macon:
WMAZ-CBS

Boise:
KIVI-ABC

Amarillo:
KAMR-NBC

Corpus Christi:
KGBT-CBS, KIII-ABC

Columbus, GA:
WTVM-ABC

La Crosse-Eau Claire:
WQOW-ABC, WXOW-ABC

Bakersfield:
KGET-NBC

Wausau-Rhinelander:
WAOW-ABC

Beaumont-Port Arthur:
KFDM-CBS

Topeka:
WIBW-CBS

Wichita Falls-Lawton:
KFDX-NBC

Erie:
WICU-NBC

Medford-Klamath Falls:
KDRV-ABC

Sioux City:
KTIV-NBC

Columbia-Jefferson City:
KOMU-NBC, KMIZ

Joplin-Pittsburg:
KSNF-NBC

Lubbock:
KCBD-NBC

Albany, GA:
WALB-NBC

Odessa-Midland:
KWES-NBC

Bangor:
WABI-CBS

Anchorage:
KTUU-NBC

Abilene-Sweetwater:
KTXS-ABC

Gainesville-Daytona Beach:
WCTV-CBS, WGFL-CBS, WPEC-CBS

Utica:
WKTV-NBC

Alexandria, LA:
KALB-NBC

Rapid City:
KNBN-NBC

Watertown:
WWTI-ABC

Lake Charles:
KPLC-NBC

Charlottesville:
WVIR-NBC

San Angelo:
KLST-CBS

Helena:
KPAX-CBS, KRTV-CBS, KTVQ-CBS, KXLF-CBS

Toronto North and Central Ontario:
CFTO-CTV

Vancouuver-Province of BC:
GLOBAL-IND

London Western Ontario:
CJOH-CTV

Ottawa-Eastern Ontario:
CJOH-CTV

Halifax-NS Maritimes:
ATV-CJCH

Edmonton-Northern Alberta:
CFRN-CTV-CTV

Calgary-Alberta:
CICT-IND

Saskatchewan:
CFSK-IND

Newfoundland:
CBNT-CBC

Hamilton:
CH-TV

RADIO STATIONS affiliated with Children's Miracle Network
Listed in alphabetical order:

CFSR
Abbotsford, British Columbia

KCDD-FM
Abilene, Texas

KLTL-FM
Abilene, Texas

KBCY-FM
Abilene, Texas

KHXS-FM
Abilene, Texas

KVRP
Abilene, Texas

KAGT-FM
Abilene, Texas

WKDD-FM
Akron, Ohio

WOBB-FM
Albany, Georgia

WGY-AM
Albany, New York

KPEK-FM
Albuquerque, New Mexico

KQID-FM
Alexandria, Louisiana

KMXJ-FM
Amarillo, Texas

KMML-FM
Amarillo, Texas

KASH-FM
Anchorage, Alaska

WHMA
Anniston, Alabama

WSTR-FM
Atlanta, Georgia

WBBQ-FM
Augusta, Georgia

WIBL-FM
Augusta, Georgia

KVET-FM
Austin, Texas

KBKO-FM
Bakersfield, California

WWMX-FM
Baltimore, Maryland

WKSQ-FM
Bangor, Maine

WNXX
Baton Rouge, Louisiana

WTGE
Baton Rouge, Louisiana

KNXX
Baton Rouge, Louisiana

KAYD-FM
Beaumont, Texas

WCIR-FM
Beckley, West Virginia

WWYL-FM
Binghamton, New York

WAAL-FM
Binghamton, New York

WNBF-FM
Binghamton, New York

WHWK-FM
Binghamton, New York

WMJJ-FM
Birmingham, Alabama

WQEN
Birmingham, Alabama

KQFC-FM
Boise, Idaho

WBMX-FM
Boston, Massachusetts

KZMY-FM
Bozeman, Montana

CKXA-FM
Brandon, Manitoba

KKQQ-FM
Brookings, South Dakota

KBRK-FM
Brookings, South Dakota

KNDE-FM
Bryan-College Station, Texas

WKSE-FM
Buffalo, New York

WOKO-FM
Burlington, Vermont

CKRY-FM
Calgary, Alberta

KHAK-FM
Cedar Rapids, Iowa

WIHB
Charleston, South Carolina

WCJZ-FM
Charlottesville, Virginia

WSUH-FM
Charlottesville, Virginia

WCYK-FM
Charlottesville, Virginia

WHTE-FM
Charlottesville, Virginia

WLYT-FM
Charlotte, North Carolina

WNGA
Chattanooga, Tennessee

WKXJ-FM
Chattanooga, Tennessee

WRXR
Chattanooga, Tennessee

WTMX-FM
Chicago, Illinois

WOJO-FM
Chicago, Illinois

WYGY-FM
Cincinnati, Ohio

WRRM-FM
Cincinnati, Ohio

WMVX-FM
Cleveland, Ohio

KATI
Columbia, Missouri

KCMQ
Columbia, Missouri

KSSZ
Columbia, Missouri

KTXY-FM
Columbia, Missouri

WTCB-FM
Columbia, South Carolina

WSNY-FM
Columbus, Ohio

WJYD
Columbus, Ohio

KRYS-FM
Corpus Christi, Texas

WKCN-FM
Columbus, Georgia

KVIL-FM
Dallas, Texas

KMXG-FM
Davenport, Iowa

WHKO-FM
Dayton, Ohio

KALC-FM
Denver, Colorado

WNIC-FM
Detroit, Michigan

WDJR-FM
Dothan, Alabama

WDBT-FM
Dothan, Alabama

WESP-FM
Dothan, Alabama

WQZY-FM
Dublin, Georgia

98FM
Dublin, Ireland

KSTZ-FM
Des Moines, Iowa

KLVY-FM
Dubuque, Iowa

KTCO-FM
Duluth, Minnesota

CISN-FM
Edmonton, Alberta

CHQT-AM
Edmonton, Alberta

CKNG-FM
Edmonton, Alberta

CHED-AM
Edmonton, Alberta

KTSM-FM
El Paso, Texas

WNKI-FM
Elmira, New York

WJET
Erie, Pennsylvania

WTWF
Erie, Pennsylvania

KODZ-FM
Eugene, Oregon

WIKY-FM
Evansville, Indiana

KMCK-FM
Fayetteville, Arkansas

WAJI-FM
Ft. Wayne, Indiana

WLAY-FM
Fargo, North Dakota

WLAY-FM
Florence-Muscle Shoals, Alabama

WLAY-AM
Florence-Muscle Shoals, Alabama

WYNA-FM
Florence-Muscle Shoals, Alabama

WYNA-AM
Florence-Muscle Shoals, Alabama

WMSR-FM
Florence-Muscle Shoals, Alabama

WMXV-FM
Florence-Muscle Shoals, Alabama

WFLS-FM
Fredericksburg, Virginia

KSKS-FM
Fresno, California

WEGX-FM
Florence, South Carolina

WDAR-FM
Florence, South Carolina

WSKY-FM
Gainesville, Florida

WKTK-FM
Gainesville Florida

KKJQ-FM
Garden City, Kansas

KFXX-FM
Garden City, Kansas

WMYI-FM
Greenville, South Carolina

KVGB-FM
Great Bend, Kansas

KVGB-AM
Great Bend, Kansas

KHOK
Great Bend, Kansas

KBGL
Great Bend, Kansas

WKSZ-FM
Green Bay-Appleton, Wisconsin

WHBY-AM
Green Bay-Appleton, Wisconsin

WECB
Green Bay-Appleton, Wisconsin

WAPL-FM
Green Bay-Appleton, Wisconsin

WNCT-FM
Greenville, North Carolina

WESC-FM
Greensville, South Carolina

WBZT-FM
Greenville, South Carolina

WOOD-FM
Grand Rapids, Michigan

CJCH-AM
Halifax, Nova Scotia

CIOO-FM
Halifax, Nova Scotia

CKOC-AM
Hamilton, Ontario

CHAM-AM
Hamilton, Ontario

CKLH-FM
Hamilton, Ontario

WMHX-FM
Harrisburg, Pennsylvania

WCAT-FM
Harrisburg, Pennsylvania

WDRC-FM
Hartford-New Haven, Connecticut

KRKF-FM
Helena, Montana

KBLL-AM
Helena, Montana

KBLL-FM
Helena, Montana

KZMT-FM
Helena, Montana

KCAP-AM
Helenna, Montana

KHPT
Houston, Texas

KKBQ
Houston, Texas

KTHT
Houston, Texas

WFMS-FM
Indianapolis, Indiana

WYOY-FM
Jackson, Mississippi

WUSJ-FM
Jackson, Mississippi

WJKK-FM
Jackson, Mississippi

WIIN-AM
Jackson, Mississippi

WWYN-FM
Jackson, Mississippi

WAPE-FM
Jacksonville, Florida

KXDG
Joplin, Missouri

KSYN
Joplin, Missouri

KJWK-FM
Joplin, Missouri

KIXQ
Joplin, Missouri

KMXV-FM
Kansas City, Missouri

CILK-FM
Kelowna, British Columbia

WWST-FM
Knoxville, Tennessee

KQEG-FM
La Crosse, Wisconsin

WLFN-AM
La Crosse, Wisconsin

WLXR-FM
La Crosse, Wisconsin

WQCC-FM
La Crosse, Wisconsin

WKOA
Lafayette, Indiana

KNGT-FM
Lake Charles, Louisiana

KHLA-FM
Lake Charles, Louisiana

WIOV-FM
Lancaster, Pennsylvania

WVIC-FM
Lansing, Michigan

WLXX-FM
Lexington, Kentucky

KZKX
Lincoln, Nebraska

KURB-FM
Little Rock, Arkansas

CIQM-FM
London, Ontario

CJBX-FM
London, Ontario

CJBX-AM
London, Ontario

KBIG-FM
Los Angeles, California

KILL-FM
Lubbock, Texas

WPEZ-FM
Macon, Georgia

KJAM-FM
Madison, South Dakota

WZEE-FM
Madison, Wisconsin

KLDZ-FM
Medford, Oregon

WMC-FM
Memphis, Tennessee

WKLH-FM
Milwaukee, Wisconsin

KSTP-FM
Minneapolis-St. Paul, Minnesota

WMXC-FM
Mobile, Alabama

CJMO
Moncton, New Brunswick

CJXL
Moncton, New Brunswick

WMXS-FM
Montgomery, Alabama

CHOM-FM
Montreal, Quebec

CJFM-FM
Montreal, Quebec

WVAQ-FM
Morgantown, West Virginia

WRVW-FM
Nashville, Tennessee

WQNZ
Natchez, Mississippi

KTGV
Natchez, Mississippi

WKSO
Natchez, Mississippi

WNAT-AM
Natchez, Mississippi

WTKL-FM
New Orleans, Louisiana

WSMB-AM
New Orleans, Louisiana

WLMG-FM
New Orleans, Louisiana

WKBU-FM
New Orleans, Louisiana

WEZB-FM
New Orleans, Louisiana

WWL-AM
New Orleans, Louisiana

KHKX-FM
Odessa-Midland, Texas

KQRX-FM
Odessa-Midland, Texas

KTXC-FM
Odessa-Midland, Texas

KXXY-FM
Oklahoma City, OK

KXKT-FM
Omaha, Nebraska

WMGF-FM
Orlando, Florida

CKBY-FM
Ottawa, Ontario

CKQB-FM
Ottawa, Ontario

WYYX
Panama City, Florida

WYOO-FM
Panama City, Florida

WPBG-FM
Peoria, Illinois

WOGL-FM
Philadelphia, Pennsylvania

KMLE-FM
Phoenix, Arizona

WFNK-FM
Portland, Maine

KWJJ-FM
Portland, Oregon

WAVT-FM
Pottsville, Pennsylvania

CKDV-FM
Prince George, British Columbia

WWKX
Providence, Rhode Island

WWLI-FM
Providence, Rhode Island

WSKO-FM
Providence, Rhode Island

WSKO-AM
Providence, Rhode Island

WRAL-FM
Raleigh-Durham, North Carolina

CFWF-FM
Regina, Saskatchewan

CKRM-AM
Regina, Saskatchewan

CHMX-FM
Regina, Saskatchewan

WMXB-FM
Richmond-Petersburg, Virginia

WSLC
Roanoke, Virginia

WVOR-FM
Rochester, New York

KWOD
Sacramento, California

KRXQ-FM
Sacramento, California

KDND-FM
Sacramento, California

KSSJ
Sacramento, California

WIOG-FM
Saginaw, Michigan

KILS-FM
Salina, Kansas

KQNS-FM
Salina, Kansas

KXTN-FM
San Antonio, Texas

KLSD-AM
San Diego, California

KUSS-FM
San Diego, California

KMYI-FM
San Diego, California

KSEG-FM
Sacramento, California

KOCN-FM
Salinas, California

KIXY-FM
San Angelo, Texas

KWFR-FM
San Angelo, Texas

KSAN-FM
San Francisco-Oakland, California

CJMK-FM
Saskatoon, Saskatchewan

WGZO-FM
Savannah, Georgia

WGZR-FM
Savannah, Georgia

KBKS-FM
Seattle-Tacoma, Washington

WZZB-AM
Seymour, Indiana

WOKC-FM
Seymour, Indiana

KGLI-FM
Sioux City, Iowa

KTWB
Sioux Falls, South Dakota

WDBR-FM
Springfield, Illinois

WMAS-AM
Springfield-Holyoke, Massachusetts

WMAS-FM
Springfield-Holyoke, Massachusetts

KOMG-FM
Springfield, Missouri

KIXZ-FM
Spokane, Washington

CKSJ-FM
St. John's, Newfoundland

KEZK
St. Louis, Missouri

WKOK-AM
Sunbury, Pennsylvania

WQKX-FM
Sunbury, Pennsylvania

WYYY
Syracuse, New York

WBBS-FM
Syracuse, New York

WSYR-AM
Syracuse, New York

WWHT-FM
Syracuse, New York

WTLY-FM
Tallahassee, Florida

KUSJ-FM
Temple, Texas

CHTM-AM
Thompson, Manitoba

CJEZ-FM
Toronto, Ontario

CKFM-FM
Toronto, Ontario

CFRB-AM
Toronto, Ontario

WAEZ-FM
Tri-Cities, Tennessee

KRQQ-FM
Tucson, Arizona

WTXT-FM
Tuscaloosa, Alabama

KWEN-FM
Tulsa, Oklahoma

WWZD-FM
Tupelo, Mississippi

KMOO-FM
Tyler-Longview, Texas

KTYL-FM
Tyler, Texas

WLZW-FM
Utica, New York

CISL-AM
Vancouver, British Columbia

CKZZ-FM
Vancouver, British Columbia

CFMI-FM
Vancouver, British Columbia

CIOC-FM
Victoria, British Columbia

WPTE-FM
Virginia Beach, Virginia

KSDR-AM
Watertown, South Dakota

KSDR-FM
Watertown, South Dakota

WRMF-FM
West Palm Beach, Florida

CKMM-FM
Winnipeg, Manitoba

CFQX-FM
Winnipeg, Manitoba

WMMJ-FM
Washington, District of Columbia

WKYS
Washington, District of Columbia

WBDI-FM
Watertown, New York

WYTE
Wausau, Wisconsin

WHUD-FM
Westchester, New York

KZSN
Wichita, Kansas

KLUR-FM
Wichita Falls, Texas

KOLI-FM
Wichita Falls, Texas

WASH-FM
Washington, District of Columbia

WMGS-FM
Wilkes Barre-Scranton,
Pennsylvania

WBHT-FM
Wilkes Barre-Scranton,
Pennsylvania

WKSB-FM
Williamsport, Pennsylvania

KZTS-AM
Yakima, Washington

KZTB-FM
Yakima, Washington

KZTA-FM
Yakima, Washington

KYXE-AM
Yakima, Washington

KFFM-FM
Yakima, Washington

KIT-AM
Yakima, Washington

WHOT-FM
Youngstown, Ohio

BOARD MEMBERS

The following individuals have rendered invaluable service to Children's Miracle Network as members of the Board of Trustees, 1983-2018:

Chairman of the Board:

J. Gary Sheets, President,
Coordinated Financial Services

Brett Hutchens, Principal,
Casto Southeast Realty

Dr. Randall L. O'Donnell, CEO,
Arkansas Children's Hospital

Alan Brass, CEO,
St. Louis Children's Hospital

Jon Vice, CEO,
Children's Hospital of Wisconsin

Diana Morgan,
The Walt Disney Company

Dr. Bill Neal, Chairman,
Department Peds U.W.V.C.H.

Dr. Jim Dearth, CEO,
Alabama Children's Hospital

Tom Sargent, President,
First Tech Credit Union

Mario Pelozzi, President,
Walmart Canada

Steve Weisz, President,
Marriott Vacation Clubs

Nana Mensah, CEO, 'Xports Inc.

John Bozard, President,
Arnold Palmer Children's Hospital
Foundation

Grady Rosier
Blair L. Sadler
Mary Sammons
Gary H. See
Dennis Sexton
John Schneider
Horace H. Sibley
Michael Simmons
Fred Smith
Hyrum Smith
Jeff Smith
Don Soderquist

Jeff Sperring
Tom Sullivan
Walter W. Sullivan, Jr.
Andrea Thomas
Alan K. Tibbitts
Maurice Tousson
Stuart Turgel
Debbye Turner
Mark Van Wagoner
Joseph Viviano
Frank J. Vuono
Harold H. Williams

The following individuals have rendered invaluable service to Children's Miracle Network on the Board of Governors:

Charlie E. Amato
Jean Birch
Carolyn F. Bivens
Cathy Burns
Gary Buroker
Kane Calamari
Paul V. Carlucci
Stuart Clark
Robert L. Colman
Carlton L. Curtis
Jim Dearth
Diane Doniger
Peter Ferrara
Jeff Friedman
George Habib
James L. Hall
Don Harris
Tim Hawley
Susan Henderson
David Heppner
Stan Hollen

Brett Hutchens
Jennifer Jean
Michael Keller
Greg Kennedy
Mitch Koch
Marilyn McCoo
Drayton McLane
Jenny Love Meyer
Michael G. Mischler
Wenda Harris Millard
George Mohachi
Dianna Morgan
Merlin Olsen
Glenn Plumby
Joe Portera
Mike Reagan
Jerry I. Reitman
Mary Lou Retton
Mike K. Roemer
Steve A. Rum
Tom Sargent

Don Semmler
Curtis Silwa
Tom E. Smith
Don Soderquist
John T. Standley
Rob Steigerwald
Celia Swanson
Vinnie Tracey

Joseph Viviano
Frank Vuono
Edward A. Watson
Stephen P. Weisz
Patricia M. Wyatt
Steve Young
Mike Youngblood

YOU GOTTA BE KIDDING!

Index